WITHDRAWN
UTSA LIBRARIES

PSYCHOTHERAPEUTIC
METAPHORS

A Guide to Theory and Practice

BRUNNER/MAZEL
BASIC PRINCIPLES INTO PRACTICE SERIES
Series Editor: Natalie H. Gilman

The *Brunner/Mazel Basic Principles Into Practice Series* is designed to present—in a series of concisely written, easily understandable volumes—the basic theory and clinical principles associated with a variety of disciplines and types of therapy. These volumes will serve not only as "refreshers" for practicing therapists, but also as basic texts on the college and graduate level.

**BRUNNER/MAZEL
BASIC PRINCIPLES INTO PRACTICE SERIES
VOLUME 5**

PSYCHOTHERAPEUTIC METAPHORS

A Guide to Theory and Practice

PHILIP BARKER

Professor, Departments of Psychiatry and Paediatrics
University of Calgary

Director, Department of Psychiatry
Alberta Children's Hospital, Calgary

BRUNNER/MAZEL *Publishers* ● NEW YORK

Library of Congress Cataloging-in-Publication Data

Barker, Philip.
    Psychotherapeutic metaphors: a guide to theory and practice/
Philip Barker.
        p.   cm.—(Brunner/Mazel basic principles into practice
series; v. 5)
    Includes bibliographical references and index.
    ISBN 0-87630-776-4 (pbk.)
    1. Metaphor—Therapeutic use. 2. Psychotherapy. I. Title.
II. Series.
    [DNLM: 1. Psychotherapy—methods. 2. Communication. WM 420
B2553p 1996]
RC489.M47B368   1996
616.89'14—dc20
DNLM/DLC
for Library of Congress   95-20643
                                                                                                    CIP

Copyright © 1996 by Brunner/Mazel, Inc.

All rights reserved. No part of this book may
be reproduced by any process whatsoever without
the written permission of the copyright owner.

Published by
BRUNNER/MAZEL, INC.
19 Union Square West
New York, New York 10003

Manufactured in the United States of America

10   9   8   7   6   5   4   3   2   1

Library
University of Texas
at San Antonio

CONTENTS

INTRODUCTION

For much of our time, most of us communicate in a fairly direct and straightforward way. When we seek information, or want someone to do something, we usually request this directly. If we have enjoyed a movie or a vacation, we will often describe our experience as accurately as we can. In such situations, there is little need for an indirect approach, though some of us may like to wax poetic when telling of an exceptional experience—one that cannot be adequately described in mundane, everyday prose.

In some circumstances, direct communication proves ineffective and indirect communication, or what are sometimes called strategic communication devices, may achieve what the direct approach does not. We will examine these situations, and how we may approach them, in later sections of this book. Here it is only necessary to point out that the use of metaphor can be a powerful communication tool.

When confronted with a situation in which a number of people seem to be tripping over each other in carrying out a task, you might point out to those concerned that there are too many of them engaged in the endeavor. An alternative, though, is to use a proverb such as, "Too many cooks spoil the broth."

Such a proverb may make its point with greater force. But why? There are several possible reasons. First, the proverb is short and to the point and requires little explanation. Secondly, it distances the participants in the endeavor from what they are doing by offering them an illustration from another area (unless, of course, the endeavor they are engaged in is cooking). Thus, it may have added objectivity. Thirdly, it has a history: Those involved may have heard it before and may already have some acceptance of the truth within it.

It is for reasons such as these, and others we will examine later, that human beings have long employed metaphorical means of communicating with each other. These have included not only proverbs, but fairy tales, biblical stories, Greek mythology, novels, poems, drawings, and other artistic devices. Jesus Christ, surely one of the most effective communicators ever, seems rarely to have given direct answers to any serious question; his preferred response was the parable. Would his teaching have survived 2000 years if it had been couched in direct, rather than metaphorical, language? One wonders.

In the process of psychotherapy, effective communication between therapist and client is a basic requirement. Without it, there is little possibility of the treatment being effective. Metaphors are just one of the means whereby we can, when we need to, increase the effectiveness with which we communicate. This says nothing special about psychotherapy, though, for metaphors are used in many situations in which people seek to communicate effectively with each other—for example, teaching, selling, and administration.

Metaphorical communication is sometimes referred to as a "strategic" device. It is one of a number of such devices that may be employed in the course of psychotherapy. It is a valuable tool and one that all psychotherapists, regardless of their theoretical background or clinical approach, should be able to press into use when the occasion arises. This book will examine its various uses and the many ways in which it may be applied.

A word of caution is in order, however. Psychotherapy cannot be learned from books. Books can enhance one's skills and suggest new approaches, but there is no substitute, certainly, for properly supervised clinical experience. Good books can enhance such supervision—and I hope this one will do just that—but they cannot replace it.

PSYCHOTHERAPEUTIC METAPHORS

A Guide to Theory and Practice

1

METAPHORS IN HUMAN COMMUNICATION

A story is told of an ancient King of Egypt who lost his eyesight. His doctors could not cure him. Then a physician from the East arrived. After examining the King, he said he could prepare an ointment, made from a golden-headed fish swimming somewhere in the sea, that would restore the King's eyesight.

Every fishing vessel was pressed into service and many fish were caught. But none had a golden head. Then, on the final day before the physician must leave, the King's son decided to cast his net into the water once more. To his amazement, in his net he saw a fish with a golden head. "Quick," he said to himself, "I must take this fish to the palace before the physician returns to his home." But as he was placing the fish in a bowl of water, the fish looked up at him with sad, pleading eyes. Suddenly, he knew that he must spare the fish's life. He threw it back into the sea.

When the King heard of this, he was angry and condemned his son to death. But the Queen decided she must save the prince's life. Dressing him in ordinary clothes, and filling his pockets with gold coins, she put him on a ship that was sailing to a distant land.

As he was leaving, she gave him one last piece of advice: "Do not employ any servant who wants to be paid every month."

The prince thought his mother's advice strange, but long experience had taught him that what she advised always proved sound.

At last the ship arrived at its destination—a beautiful land with forests, fields and neat houses. The prince fell in love with the place and bought one of the houses.

Many servants offered their services, but all asked to be paid monthly. Then, one day an Arab came, imploring the prince to hire him.

"I do not seek money," the Arab said. "Please wait until the end of the year and then decide what my services have been worth to you." The prince knew he must hire him.

On the other side of the mountains that bordered the land, there was a desert ravaged by a sea monster. The ruler of the land had many times sent soldiers to ambush and kill the monster, but they had always fallen asleep before the monster had appeared. Punishing the soldiers had not solved the problem.

Eventually, the ruler proclaimed a large reward for anyone who killed the monster. So the Arab went to the ruler and asked, "If my master slays the monster, what reward will you give him?"

"Whatever he desires," answered the ruler.

That night, the Arab covered himself with an ointment that made his skin itch so severely that it was impossible for him to go to sleep. He waited, hiding behind a huge rock. In due course, the monster appeared out of the sea. It was hideous—part bird, part beast and part serpent. It moved steadily forward, passing over the rock where the Arab was waiting. At just the right moment, the Arab jumped up and plunged his dagger into the flesh behind the monster's ear, wounding him fatally. He cut off the monster's ears and took them to his master.

"Take these to the ruler and tell him that they are the ears of the monster who was terrorizing the land on the other side of the mountain," he said.

"But it was not I that killed the monster," said the prince. "It was you."

The prince did not like taking credit for what he had not done, but the Arab prevailed upon him to do so.

The ruler was delighted and even offered the young man his daughter's hand in marriage. The prince declined, asking instead for a ship to take him to see the world. The prince and his servant visited many lands. At length, they reached a great Kingdom. The prince learned that the King's daughter was the most beautiful princess in the world and resolved to ask for her hand in marriage.

Taking with him some of the fine jewels the ruler had given him, he sought an audience with the King. With his faithful servant behind him, he presented the King with the jewels and made his request, which the King granted.

"But I must tell you," the King said, "that my daughter has already been through over one hundred marriage ceremonies and not one of the men she married lived for more than twelve hours."

The prince thought of withdrawing his request, but his trusted Arab servant prevailed upon him not to do so.

"Do not be concerned about what the King says, but take his daughter for your bride," his servant told him.

So the prince told the King, "Luck must change some time, and who would not risk his life for the hand of one so perfect as your daughter?"

The wedding took place that very evening. After the marriage, the prince and his bride retired to their chamber. It was a clear, moonlit night and the prince walked over to the window. Suddenly, he saw a shroud lying on the ground. On it were embroidered his initials and beside it two men were digging a long and narrow hole. Suddenly the prince realized what it was—it was his grave!

Speechless and afraid, the prince turned slowly towards his bride. At that moment, a small black snake darted out of the princess' mouth and wriggled towards him. But the Arab had hidden himself in the room, suspecting that something of this sort would happen. Quick as lightning, he seized the serpent with a pair of pincers he held in his left hand, while he cut off its head with a knife.

The King was amazed next morning to find that his new son-in-law was still alive.

"I was sure that luck would turn some day," said the prince.

After that, the princess and her new husband lived happily together, hunting, sailing, and playing.

One day, a messenger arrived bringing news that the prince's father, the King of Egypt, had died and the prince had been proclaimed King. His mother asked that he return at once. The prince told his father-in-law and the King was delighted to discover that his son-in-law was the King of a great country. He ordered a ship to be made ready to take the young couple home.

When the couple arrived home, the Queen was over-joyed to see her son once more. So, too, were the people, who had suffered great hardships under their former ruler. The new King soon found himself busy with the affairs of state. He was very happy in his new life, until one day his faithful Arab servant came to him and said he must leave.

The young King was dismayed.

"Surely you will not leave me after all we have been through together," he said.

"Alas, I must," his servant replied. "I have received a summons that I dare not disobey."

"In that case, I cannot keep you. But please take with you everything I have that you desire, for without your help I should have long ago been dead."

"And without you," replied the Arab, "I also would have been dead, for I am the golden-headed fish."

Fairy tales are but one variety of metaphor. They offer the reader or the listener messages, which are presented indirectly. The fairy tale above is but one of many that could have been quoted. What are its merits? While they are no more and no less than those of many other tales, examining them may show how effective they can be as both subtle and elegant means of making points. At the same time, they can be entertaining and if, for some reason, the reader or listener fails to take the points the tale aspires to make, little has been lost. Indeed something may have been gained if the tale has provided enjoyment.

The main point the tale of *The Golden-Headed Fish* makes is obvious enough—one good deed is often repaid by other good deeds done in return. Surely, though, it makes that point more powerfully than the simple statement in the foregoing sentence! It does so in part because of its greater length—though the version above is much abbreviated. As the tale unfolds, the reader may wonder what will happen next and, in particular, what the connection is between the prince's adventures after he flees from the wrath of his father and the experiences he has subsequently. The, perhaps unexpected, "punch line" at the end then makes its point with special force.

Along the way, the story makes many other points. It illustrates, without overt mention, the virtues of loyalty and trust. It also suggests that we may benefit by taking the advice of our mothers and, probably by extension, that of others who care about us and are older and wiser—even when the advice seems strange and its value is difficult to comprehend. It extols the expression of gratitude, and advocates original approaches to difficult and resistant problems—as illustrated by the Arab's idea of covering himself with an irritant ointment to keep him awake while he awaited the arrival of the sea monster. It does all these things without directly giving any advice or making any suggestions. The wealth of fairy tales that is our common heritage and the fascination they hold for many people are surely evidence of their value.

There is nothing new about the use of metaphor in human communication. The oldest known major recorded work of literature is the epic tale, *Gilgamesh*. This was written on clay tablets in cuneiform (that is, wedge-shaped script) at least 1300 years before Homer recounted the *Iliad*. The first of these tablets was discovered when, during the excavation of Ninevah starting in 1845, the library of Ashurbanipal, the last great King of Assyria, was discovered. Many versions of this story, in a variety of languages, have been discovered since then. It is believed by scholars that the adventures of Gilgamesh were first written down about 2100 B.C. (Rosenberg, 1986). The epic is too long by far to be recounted here, but it is probably not by chance that this oldest surviving piece of literature contains many messages conveyed metaphorically.

Gilgamesh is a tale of temptation by Ishtar, perhaps the earliest recorded *femme fatale*; of fights with monsters; of the quest for immortality or eternal youth; of friendship and the pain we suffer when our friendships are ended by death; of how we can often achieve with the help of others that which we could not do on our own.

Writing of *Gilgamesh*, Rosenberg (1986) suggests that:

> ...it reaffirms the similarities in human nature and human values across time and space [and it] reveals the importance of friendship and love, pride and honor, adventure and accomplishment, and also the fear of death and the wish for immortality.... (p. 182)

What struck me on reading *Gilgamesh* was how little has changed in the last 4000 years. On Saturday mornings, our children may sit in front of their television sets and watch the present-day heroes—the Power Rangers, Batman, or Teenage Mutant Ninja Turtles—defeating monsters of one sort or another. The powers of good and evil and the clashes between them are depicted in the metaphors of the 1990s, but the messages have not changed much. The possibility, even the inevitability, of good overcoming evil; the value of friendships and loyalty; the fear of death—all are much the same today as in 2100 B.C.

The story of *Gilgamesh* is worth reading, not just because it is the oldest major literary work of which we know, but because of the powerful way it makes its points. How much more power such tales have than, for example, simple statements that "love and friendship are important!"

The literature of the world is replete with tales that carry their message through the power of metaphor. The authors whose work is preserved in the Bible used metaphor to the fullest. The Book of Job, one of the Bible's oldest books, is surely a metaphor for the relationship between God and people. Many biblical metaphors, for example, the story of "David and Goliath" or the parable of "The Good Samaritan," have been powerful enough and have had enough continuing relevance to the human condition that they have become a part of our everyday language. Greek mythology, fairy tales, and proverbs all convey meaning, often very powerfully, metaphorically.

Stories and other metaphorical devices may suggest ideas subliminally. Many authors, for example, Watzlawick (1978) and Mills and Crowley (1986), believe that they are ways of communicating with the "right brain"—that is, the right cerebral hemisphere.

There is evidence that the two cerebral hemispheres process information in different ways (Sperry, 1968). These have been linked to the "two languages," about which Watzlawick (1978) writes as follows:

> There are thus two languages involved. The one, in which for instance this sentence is expressed, is objective, definitional, cerebral, logical, analytic; it is the language of reason, of science, explanation and interpretation, and therefore the language of most psychotherapy. The other...is much more difficult to define—precisely because it is not the language of definition. We might call it the language of imagery, of metaphor, or *pars pro toto*, perhaps of symbols, but certainly of synthesis and totality, and not of analytical dissection. (pp. 14–15)

It is widely believed that these two languages are processed in, respectively, the left and the right hemispheres of the brain. For the practicing psychotherapist, however, the anatomical and neurological basis of this may be less important than the knowledge that the two types of language exist. This concept helps explain why, when people clearly understand intellectually (that is, with their "left

brain," if we accept the above hypothesis) that a certain
course of action is advisable, they nevertheless often find
themselves compelled by forces outside their conscious
control to take a different course—and one that may have
unsatisfactory results. All this is discussed further by
Watzlawick (1978) in *The Language of Change*. Metaphors, such as the fairy tale above, are thought to bypass
the "left brain," which is seen as a sort of logical watchdog
standing guard over what we take in, aiming to ensure that
we behave in a rational fashion. Sometimes, when changes
are needed in the functioning of the "right brain," we need
to find ways of bypassing this watchdog.

How do metaphors do this? Well, we all know that fairy
tales are not true. They are stories from an imaginary
world, told to children for fun. So the logical watchdog is
put off guard. There is no need to question the veracity of
fairy tales. No one is really claiming that what they recount
actually happened; if it did, it was long ago and does not
apply to our present day. In reality, though, they carry
messages that can be applied to our present situation—
messages that are as relevant today as they were in the
distant past.

Metaphor is a feature of modern literature no less than
it is of ancient writings, and there can be few more brilliant
examples than George Orwell's *Animal Farm* (1945). Without even a mention of the Russian revolution and the
"communist" regime that followed it, the book describes
and gives us insight into what happened—and what went
wrong. It illustrates with telling force how the lofty ideals
of many of the original revolutionaries were lost. Reread-
ing it as I prepared to write this book, I was filled with
sadness and compassion for the fate of the unfortunate
animals who rebelled in a blow for what they believed
would be freedom. "All animals are equal" was at first the
rallying cry, but it soon turned out that some animals were
more equal than others—the "some," of course, being the
pigs. Such is the power of Orwell's writing that I, at least,
found myself moved with as much compassion for the
animals as I have ever been for the victims of Stalin's

purges. Please consider a reading of *Animal Farm* as a necessary part of the process of learning about therapeutic metaphors.

Metaphor is not confined to written compositions. Meaning can be conveyed metaphorically in drawings, paintings, and sculptures. Political cartoonists are especially skilled at communicating by metaphor. Indeed, why would anyone bother to draw, or at least publish, cartoons commenting on the doings of politicians if they had no advantage over simple statements in prose?

Later in this book we will also learn something of the brilliant work of Mills and Crowley (1986) who have developed to a fine art the use of what they term "artistic metaphors."

SUMMARY

Metaphors have been used as aids to human communication as far back as history takes us. Epic stories, as well as contemporary novels and short stories, can carry powerful messages that may help readers and listeners acquire new perspectives on their own life situations or on almost any other issue.

It seems that the power of metaphor derives from its ability to convey meaning to the part of the brain that deals with imagery, symbols, and people's overall view of the world—often considered to be located in the right cerebral hemisphere. It seems to bypass the logical, analytic, rational aspects of our thinking—often identified with the left cerebral hemisphere. The latter seems to lack the creativity needed to come up with innovative responses to some challenges—those that do not respond to logical analysis.

2

THE USE OF
METAPHORS IN
PSYCHOTHERAPY

Early in the course of the Second World War, the French and their allies, in preparation for an attack by the German armed forces, constructed a massive complex of fortifications along the border between France and Germany. This was named the Maginot Line. It was thought to be impregnable—and maybe it was.

At its northern end, the Maginot Line met the border between France and Belgium, at which point it petered out. The French did not consider it necessary to fortify heavily their border with Belgium, which was not seen as a potential enemy. There may have been an assumption that Hitler had no quarrel with Belgium; therefore, that country would not be involved in any war that might break out. How wrong the French and their allies were! Maybe Hitler had no special quarrel with Belgium, but he had no compunction about sending his army through the virtually undefended Belgian borders to outflank the allies. This left no need for an attack on the Maginot Line, which became irrelevant. A successful military strategy! The French and their allies were the victims of unimaginative thinking based on old fashioned concepts of war.

WHAT IS METAPHOR?

The essence of metaphor is the use of one thing to represent another. As Turbayne (1970), drawing from Aristotle, puts it:

> Metaphor consists in giving the thing a name that belongs to something else; the transference being either from genus to species or from species to species, or on the grounds of analogy. (p. 11)

Metaphor need not be expressed in words. Pictures can carry meaning metaphorically, as we have seen political cartoons seek to do. So may statues and memorials such as the tomb of the unknown soldier. The Voortrekker monument in South Africa, a remarkable monument to the struggle of those Boers who made the long trek from Cape Province to the area around Pretoria, has powerful symbolic meaning. So, too, has the wall in Washington, D.C., on which are inscribed the names of those killed in the Vietnam conflict. How much more such symbols say than countless words do!

WHY SHOULD WE USE METAPHORS?

But why should therapists, or others who want to refine their communication skills, take the trouble to study the use of metaphors? What's wrong with just saying what we want to say and leaving it at that? Basically, there is nothing wrong with saying what we mean in plain language—except that it does not always yield the desired results. In some situations, whether during psychotherapy or in other endeavors, direct communication may prove entirely satisfactory, but we must nevertheless be prepared with other options to which we can turn when direct communication proves ineffective.

It is not simply that our clients may not always accept, or even believe, what we and others tell them. Often they do believe that the advice they are given is sound, yet they remain unable to make the needed changes in their behavior or feelings. We may advise the abusive father to stop beating his child, but he may not do as we suggest. He may understand—intellectually—the good sense behind the advice we give, but that does not stop his angry feelings getting the better of him when his child engages in certain activities; some fathers may refuse even to accept that the advice is sound. They may have a deeply felt, sincere conviction that, under certain circumstances, physical punishment is appropriate. When their angry emotions rise up within them, such fathers may be unable to control them.

THE STRATEGIC APPROACH

How, then, are we to help to promote change in situations such as the above? More subtle, creative approaches are needed; these are often called "strategic" approaches. Skill in their use is what distinguishes the expert, well-trained psychotherapist from the everyday purveyor of good advice.

We are not, of course, talking only of how we may help stop parents beating their children. We are talking as much of the alcoholic who cannot stop drinking despite the conscious awareness of its damaging effects—and of the one who is not fully aware of these effects. And we are talking of the person who, despite conscious awareness of his or her talents and accomplishments, still has deep-seated feelings of inadequacy or low self-esteem. We are talking of the woman who is aware of the drawbacks of returning to her abusive husband but, despite conscious realization that to return is unwise and will likely lead to more abuse, nevertheless feels compelled to return by some force of which she has little understanding and over which she has no control. Simply advising that abused spouse to leave the man who has repeatedly abused her may not be enough. It often is not.

A myriad of other clinical—and nonclinical—examples could be given of situations in which direct approaches and the working of the rational, logical (or "left brain") part of the mind often do not result in the subject resolving his or her dilemma. Perhaps, though, the examples above are enough for now.

A general, planning a military operation, is often confronted with the choice of mounting a frontal attack or outflanking the enemy. Hitler and his generals chose the outflanking option in the face of the Maginot Line. While I do not regard my clients as "the enemy," there is something to be learned from this metaphor. Sometimes, the direct, frontal approach is not the best one. Our Maginot Lines or psychological fortifications—often called, as military fortifications are, "defenses"—are too powerful.

THE RANGE OF STRATEGIC APPROACHES

Metaphor is but one of a number of strategic devices that may be used to help promote the change that is the objective of all psychotherapy. The number of possible strategies we may use is probably infinite, being limited only by the boundaries of our creativity. There are, however, some established approaches that have been well described and are widely used. I have listed some of the main strategic therapeutic interventions elsewhere (Barker, 1992) but, in order to place metaphor in context, they are reviewed here. They include:

Reframing and positive connotation

There is probably an element of reframing in all strategic therapeutic devices (Barker, 1994). As an example of reframing, we may take the behavior of the parent who physically punishes a child to such an extent that it amounts to abuse. This may be reframed as a commendable attempt to correct the child's antisocial behavior. The therapeutic task, then, becomes one of finding better, nonabusive ways of achieving the same end.

Another example is "developmental reframing" (Coppersmith, 1981) in which children's, and especially adolescents', difficult behavior is reframed as "childish" rather than "bad." Being confronted with the interpretation that his violence and outbursts of temper are more like the behavior of a toddler may have a salutary effect on the responses of an acting-out teenage boy. We will return to the subject of reframing when we consider how metaphors may do this.

The use of metaphors

More than most strategic interventions, metaphorical approaches may be regarded as outflanking maneuvers. The "left brain" is outflanked, as we discussed above. Another way of looking at how metaphors work is to use the analogy of entering a place in disguise. The ideas, the suggestions as to how change may be promoted, are disguised in a story, an anecdote, a cartoon, or some other metaphoric communication.

Giving paradoxical directives

These include both instructions that change would be unwise or that changes should be made only very slowly. I have mentioned elsewhere (Barker, 1992, pp. 184–185) the case of a family in which the 19-year-old daughter was acting out in a variety of irresponsible ways and leaving her parents to care for her illegitimate son. After mentioning how they could take the firmer stand with her that seemed to be required, I then advised against such action, saying that their love for their daughter seemed too great and that I thought it would be too upsetting for them to do this. I expressed doubts about whether they would ever be able to follow through with the plan I had outlined. This stimulated the parents to take exactly the line I had advised against.

Prescribing rituals and other tasks

These usually have metaphorical significance and are really a subgroup of metaphors. There are many examples in *Rituals in Families and Family Therapy* (Imber-Black, Roberts, & Whiting, 1988). One of these is the ritual use of objects to celebrate the termination of therapy. Imber-Black et al. (1988, p. 82) describe how the therapist presented two objects to the family of a girl who had had an eating disorder—a potato (symbolizing the potato chips which were the girl's favorite food) and a kiwi fruit (which the girl hated). These were to be frozen and kept in the freezer. Then, when any member of the family felt that a discussion was needed, the two items were to be brought out. When they had thawed out, a family meeting would be held. The objects thus came to be symbols of the work the family had done—metaphors for and reminders of the therapy that had been completed.

Declaring therapeutic impotence

It sometimes happens that the therapist gets into a symmetrical "battle" with the client. Each idea or suggestion the therapist may offer is rejected as impractical, unacceptable, or having been tried previously without success. The client or family may seem to be trying to "defeat" all the therapist's attempts to help. In such cases, declaring oneself impotent and saying that one can think of nothing further that might be helpful—or even saying that the problems seem impossible to solve—challenges the client to come up with his or her own solutions. The fact that the client attends, even for the "useless" therapy, is usually an indication that there is some motivation for change. Then, when the therapist makes a further appointment (as is advisable), and the client accepts the appointment, this may indicate, by implication, that both therapist and client do indeed believe, at some level, that change is possible.

Prescribing interminable therapy

This may stimulate clients to take on the responsibility for making changes themselves. Like declaring impotence, this is one of the devices discussed by Palazzoli and her colleagues (1978).

Using humor

Making a situation look funny may lead to a changed perception of it—that is, a reframing. This was a technique sometimes used by Frankl (1960) who, for example, might get his obsessive-compulsive patients to laugh at their need to go back repeatedly to check that they had locked the house door.

Using a consultation group as a "Greek chorus"

This technique has been described by Papp (1980). A group of colleagues watching a family in treatment from behind a one-way mirror sends in messages from time to time. These may be messages of support, "public opinion polls" (reporting on the odds of the family changing), messages designed to surprise or confuse, messages disagreeing with the therapist (an example of the use of paradoxical directives), or messages offering advice from outside the circle of therapist and family.

Staging a debate

This is a development of the "Greek chorus," the main difference being that the "strategic team" comes out from behind the one-way screen. It then debates the situation in front of the family with the aim of offering new ways of looking at the situation and of possibly promoting change.

Externalizing the problem

This approach was advocated by White and Epston (1990). This identifies the problem—for example, "Mr. Fear" or "The Worry Bug"— as something that has taken temporary control of the individual. In a sense, "The Worry Bug" becomes a metaphor. Treatment then becomes a matter of dealing with "Mr. Fear" or whatever the externalized object may be.

"Storied therapy"

This is another device suggested by White and Epston (1990). This includes the writing of letters to clients. Many examples of such letters are to be found in White and Epston's (1990) book *Narrative Means to Therapeutic Ends*. These may lead to the awarding of certificates, such as "The Monster-Tamer and Fear-Catcher Certificate" and "Escape from Tantrums Certificate." (It is, perhaps, interesting to note here that White and Epston (1990) tackle the problem of how we are to deal with the monsters we face much as the epic poem, *Gilgamesh*, (see Chapter 1) did 4000 years ago. Had White and Epston lived in those ancient days, they might have awarded Gilgamesh a "Monster-Tamer" or even a "Monster-Destroyer" Certificate!)

The above list is not exhaustive and the various approaches are not mutually exclusive. Most of them may be seen as employing metaphorical concepts, though that does depend on how far one extends the definition of "metaphor."

THE VALUE OF TELLING STORIES IN THE PROCESS OF PSYCHOTHERAPY

We must now consider how telling stories may help promote change, especially when more direct approaches have proved unsuccessful.

Zeig (1980), in his helpful introduction to *A Teaching Seminar with Milton H. Erickson,* lists the following clinical uses of anecdotes in psychotherapy (pp. 7–15). While there are other forms of metaphor, this list covers many of the uses of metaphors of all types:

Making or illustrating points

The story of the Maginot Line is an example. It makes the point that an indirect strategy may often be preferable to a direct "frontal assault." Many proverbs make their points in succinct and telling ways. "Too many cooks spoil the broth" may be a more effective way of putting over the point that when too many people are involved in the same endeavor this may result in inferior performance. The camel is often spoken of as a horse designed by a committee!

Peseschkian's (1986) book *Oriental Stories as Tools in Psychotherapy* is full of stories, many of them quite brief, that make points concisely and effectively. I like the one about the woman who had invited the son of the founder of the Baha'i religion to dinner. When she brought out the food, she found herself apologizing for the fact that it was burnt, but explained that she had been praying that the meal would be successful. Her guest commended her for praying, but suggested that the next time she was in the kitchen she use the cookbook in her prayers!

Suggesting solutions to problems

The story of the Maginot Line is a simple example of how we might suggest that an outflanking operation is often preferable to a frontal assault on a problem. I find it is sometimes helpful to tell stories about how other clients have solved problems similar to those that the clients are currently facing. It is important to avoid breaching any confidences and sometimes the accounts I give are composites of several cases, with names and other identifying data always changed.

Helping people to recognize themselves

The therapist confronted by a person feeling depressed might tell a story about a depressed person who thought her situation was hopeless but found out that this was a result more of her state of mind that of the reality of her situation. This would probably not cure the depression, but it might provide a glimmer of insight and open the subject's mind to the possibility that things are not as bad as they seem.

Those who have reached a point of despair might be told of others who were about to give up on an enterprise when suddenly they spotted "the light at the end of the tunnel"— itself a useful metaphor. It often turns out that things are not as fixed and hopeless as they seem. An example I have found useful is the sudden collapse of the "Berlin Wall" and of the communist regimes in Eastern Europe, which caught many people by surprise. The recent dramatic changes in South Africa are another example of a sudden and—by many—unexpected turn of events. Can Nelson Mandela really have expected, during his long years in jail, that one day he would be the president of his country and that his vice-president would be a white man and a member of the party that had jailed him?

Seeding ideas and increasing motivation

Motivational problems are common among those seeking psychotherapeutic help. Such individuals may lack the motivation to engage or persist in activities they need to carry out in their life generally; or they may lack the motivation to engage effectively in psychotherapy, expecting a "magical cure" without the hard work sometimes needed in the course of therapy. For such clients, telling stories about others who lacked motivation (whether because they did not believe they could succeed or because they thought that what they were being asked to do would not work anyway) yet who did persevere and succeed may be helpful.

For those of the Jewish and Christian faiths, the story of the 40 long years the Israelites spent in the wilderness before reaching the promised land can carry powerful meaning. Moses and Aaron had a hard time keeping their dispirited and rebellious people going but eventually they did reach the "land flowing with milk and honey."

Controlling the therapeutic relationship

It is generally best if the therapist, rather than the client, controls the therapeutic relationship—that is to say, determines what happens in the therapy sessions. Our clients need new inputs, new ways of looking at things. They come to us because they have not been able to come up with and operationalize the new ideas and approaches they need. If they determine what happens during the therapy and if we accept their views of the causes of their problems and of possible solutions, change becomes less likely. Yet, openly confronting clients in such situations may fail or even lead them to drop out of therapy altogether. Sometimes, telling a relevant story, or even an irrelevant one, may help the therapist gain control of the therapeutic situation.

Embedding directives

A technique used effectively by many therapists, but perhaps by none more effectively than the late Milton Erickson, is the embedding of directives or suggestions in the course of a story. Things may be said to people "in quotes" that would be discounted or rejected if said directly. However, when embedded, they often get their message through. Even if they do not, nothing is lost; the relationship between therapist and client has not been damaged, as it might have been if the suggestion had been directly addressed to the client and rejected.

For example, the therapist might tell a story during the course of which one character says to another, "Remember who you are and don't let yourself be put down by that man." This might be a message the therapist would like to address directly to the client, but saying it indirectly in a story is often more effective. It is usually best to alter one's tone of voice and/or speed of talking while delivering the words that are "in quotes" and thus to emphasize them. It seems that this technique bypasses the "left brain," that is, the logical "watchdog" that seems so often to invalidate directly delivered ideas.

Decreasing resistance

Because stories and anecdotes present ideas indirectly and, perhaps, a little at a time, they are less likely to be actively resisted. This is really an example of the "outflanking" discussed above. The delivery of messages "in quotes" is but one of the many ways resistance, or the workings of the "logical" parts of the mind, can be overcome.

Reframing and redefining problems

Several forms of reframing have been outlined above. I have suggested elsewhere (Barker, 1994) that the process of reframing is at the heart of psychotherapy. Metaphorical approaches of various types can be highly effective in reframing problem situations. They offer our clients the opportunity to see things in a different light.

Characteristics, in either our clients or their children or other relatives, that have been regarded unfavorably may be reframed as potential assets. Thus, the capacity to be a convincing liar may be reframed as valuable to the writer of fiction; or the obstinacy of a willful child may be seen as the foundation of the determination needed to succeed in many areas of life.

Ego building

People who have difficulty dealing with the world around them may be helped by stories of how others have dealt with and overcome similar problems. We all have our moments of self-doubt and uncertainty but, like the ugly duckling who was really a swan, we suddenly find that things are not as we thought. The human story is full of tales of people who found that they had powers and potential they had not thought they possessed. There are plenty to choose from. I like the story of Ida Guillory who was for many years content to be a housewife and mother. As she later explained, "My mother's old accordion was simply another object in a closet. I started playing it as a hobby in my free time" (Guillory, 1988). But once her children had grown up, Mrs. Guillory became Queen Ida and she has, for nearly 20 years, led her Bon Temps Zydeco Band. She has been awarded a Grammy and has achieved considerable commercial success as the leader of one of the foremost groups playing Cajun music.

Modeling a way of communicating

It is said that Milton Erickson observed that if you want a man to tell you about his brother you should tell him about yours. The art of storytelling seems to have suffered a setback with the advent of the cinema and in-home video entertainment. So many of us have come to rely on the "stories" served up to us by the media, rather than creating our own. This may have impoverished the quality of our interpersonal communication, in our families and in many other situations. The therapist (or educator, parent, or other potential role model) can help counter this trend by telling stories and thus illustrating their power and utility.

Reminding people of their own resources

One of Milton Erickson's principal beliefs was that his patients had within them the resources to resolve their problems. He was expert at devising and telling his patients stories that reminded them of the things they had learned in the past, including problems they had solved and difficult situations they had successfully faced up to and dealt with.

One of Erickson's devices was to announce to his patients that he was going tell them about something that
happened to them many years earlier. He would then talk
about how they learned the letters of the alphabet, about
how difficult it was at first, with the need to remember the
shapes of each of the letters and how to distinguish "d"
from "b" or "m" from "n," and so on. Learning to ride a
bicycle was also hard for them at first. But now they can do
these things without any hesitation or conscious thought.
There is so much we all have learned that we have
forgotten learning and now take for granted! The implication, of course, is that we have the capacity to learn new
things and have learned, and can learn, a lot more than
perhaps most of us give ourselves credit for.

Desensitizing people from their fears

This use of stories is not central to the subject of this
book but is a *bona fide* use of metaphor. Telling people a
series of anecdotes or stories about their phobic objects
may help them overcome their fears of such objects. This
resembles the process of systematic desensitization.

As an example, we may take the fear many people have
of snakes. This can extend to the very mention of snakes in
conversation. While the client is in a state of relaxation or,
even better, of hypnosis, the therapist may start with the
occasional mention of snakes, working up gradually to
graphic stories of encounters with snakes. The rate of
change is adjusted to the subject's responses, so that
relaxation is maintained. The end result may be that
the subject is desensitized to snakes and the phobia is
eliminated.

OTHER USES OF METAPHORS

Metaphors have many other uses. They may serve to
enrich virtually any communication process. It is no
exaggeration to say that if you are having difficulty putting
a point across to someone, it may be well to consider a

metaphorical way of framing the message. Here are some examples of other uses for metaphors:

Establishing rapport

One of the most basic requirements for successful psychotherapy is a good level of rapport between therapist and client. Rapport is not easy to define, but it is nevertheless very real. It has been given a variety of names. Karpel and Strauss (1983) referred to the process of developing rapport as that of "building working alliances." Minuchin (1974), writing about family therapy, described rapport building as the process of "joining" families.

Trust is an element of rapport, but there is more to rapport than trust. To use the neurological analogy of "right brain" versus "left brain" function, it seems to be more a right brain than a left brain matter. Otherwise, how is it that confidence tricksters, who are the ultimate experts in the development of rapport, can manage such outrageous acts as "selling" the Brooklyn Bridge to unsuspecting tourists or persuading wealthy people, who have accumulated their fortune through hard work and prudent money management, to part with it in response to what seems like an obvious swindle? Logical, rational thinking would suggest that the Brooklyn Bridge is not for sale, but once an intense rapport is established, logic may be abandoned.

As I have put it elsewhere (Barker, 1990):

> As rapport develops the participants become increasingly involved with each other. Once it is well established an interviewer or therapist can say almost anything, even quite outrageous things, without causing offense; remarks that might be construed as insulting will be taken as being meant jokingly or at least not seriously. (p. 31)

Clearly, the establishment of rapport is a basic requirement of any sound relationship, including, but not confined to, therapist–client relationships. Salespeople and lawyers arguing their cases, physicians treating their patients, or administrators dealing with their staff—all are more effective if they take care to establish rapport with those with whom they deal.

How can metaphors help in the establishment of rapport? Telling stories can be invaluable here. This applies particularly to children. Most children love stories. They tend to be familiar with storytelling, whether at home or in school. If they have enjoyed being told stories previously, either by their family or their teacher, they are likely to look favorably upon those who tell stories. It can therefore be a good move, at the outset of one's relationship with young clients, to tell a few stories. These may be selected, and their content constructed, to promote rapport. Stories of people who were frightened or did not trust those with whom they were confronted, but who found that their fears were unfounded, may be helpful.

Sometimes, I tell children about others who have been frightened but who have found, perhaps to their surprise, that coming to the clinic, hospital, or playroom is really fun (without, of course, my giving any information that could identify those children). Having on the walls pictures drawn or painted by other children or displaying the products of other children's play or modelling activities can help reinforce the message that the place the child is in is, to use jargon beloved by present-day children, "cool."

Establishing treatment goals

Many therapists believe—and I am among them—that it helps to be clear about the goals of treatment before embarking on psychotherapy or, for that matter, on just about any human endeavor. Many clients, however, do not at first accept the necessity to define objectives. Sometimes, they just seem to want "therapy" for therapy's sake. They may have an ill-defined sense of malaise or dissatisfaction with their lives, or they may have been told by someone they respect or who is in a position of authority over them that they should go for therapy. Sometimes they come asking if they need therapy; they do not in all cases really see therapy as an activity aiming to promote change.

Starting out without clear goals—whether in psychotherapy or any other activity—is a recipe, if not for failure, at least for creating a situation in which it will be impossible to know whether or not one has succeeded.

There are many ways of putting metaphorically the need to define one's objectives when dealing with people. I sometimes talk of the man (or woman if it is a woman client) who goes into, for example, a hardware store without knowing what he wants to buy. It is quite likely that the salesperson will ask him what he is looking for and it will not be very helpful if he says he does not know or, perhaps, asks the salesperson what he (the customer) needs. If he does indeed require tools of some sort, it will be necessary for him to describe the tasks he wants to accomplish with the tools he is seeking. The staff of the hardware store will then begin to have some idea how they can help him.

Yet another simple, everyday situation may be used to make a similar point. If we are setting out on a journey in a car or on foot, and if there is to be any purpose and useful outcome, we need to know where it is we wish to go. In this, it is helpful to have a map or perhaps the guidance or company of someone who knows the way to the intended destination. The map serves as a metaphor for the process of therapy, which can be long and winding, as some journeys prove to be, or quick and direct, as journeys on fine, straight highways sometimes are. The guide, of course, is the therapist. However, some journeys can be undertaken without a guide and a map may be sufficient, as many self-help books and programs seem to be.

"Programming" for success

It is generally helpful, when we terminate therapy with our clients, if we leave them with the confidence that the progress they have made will continue. Reassuring and supportive words are usually appropriate, but they may be supported by metaphors. "You're well on your way along the right road now," carries the message that the client is now on course to achieve his or her goals—a situation which, this statement implies, was not the case before.

This concept may be elaborated further by tales about the successes others have achieved as a result of learning new skills and acquiring new knowledge or the self-confidence they formerly lacked. It is often helpful to draw on one's own personal experiences, or those of others one has known or worked with, as examples of how people have continued to progress and achieve various aims after obtaining new learnings.

Implicit in this is the basic assumption—on which, incidentally Milton Erickson seemed to base much of his professional work—that we all have within us vast un-tapped and unused potential. We simply need to gain access to it to achieve goals we may have thought impos-sible for us. This is the basis of the "storehouse of learn-ings," a concept I acquired from Erickson's work. Using this concept, I have developed the following metaphorical tale, which I have found most useful.

> Life is a bit like collecting useful things. I once knew a man who had a big store cupboard in his house. He was a person who would never throw away any-thing that might possibly be useful later. And, when you think about it, just about anything *might* have some sort of use under certain circumstances. The result was that he accumulated a great number of tools, gadgets, pieces of equipment of all sorts, screws, nails, and all sorts of what some would call junk. In fact he accumulated so much, over the course of many years, that he forgot just what was in the cupboard; and when, sometimes, he un-locked the door to look for something, he often found that he had forgotten what many of the objects were originally used for. On the other hand,

there was so much there that, although it might be
hard work and take a long time, he discovered that
he could almost always find something that he
could use to do just about anything he wanted.

Sometimes, it seems to be sufficient to leave it at that, but
I find, especially during hypnotherapeutic work, that it
can be productive to associate the idea of the storehouse of
tools and gadgets with our "unconscious storehouse of
learnings"—this being all the things we have learned over
the years but have forgotten we have learned. This theme
was much beloved by Erickson, as we shall see.

A bonus

One of the greatest advantages of communicating through
metaphors is that they are much less likely to have adverse
results than direct statements. As we have seen, statements
can even be addressed to people "in quotes." That is to say,
if you believe that it would be helpful for a client to go and
speak directly to someone on a certain subject, you may
incorporate the words you want to address to your client
in a story in which they are used by one character, speaking
to another.

SOURCES OF INFORMATION ON
THERAPEUTIC METAPHORS

Several books are available that have as their main focus
the use of metaphors in psychotherapy. *Using Metaphors
in Psychotherapy* (Barker, 1985) discusses some of the
theoretical ideas and general principles underlying the use
of metaphors, and goes on to suggest ways in which
metaphorical approaches may be used in a variety of
clinical situations.

Therapeutic Metaphors for Children and the Child Within
(Mills & Crowley, 1986) is a valuable work that makes
considerable use of many of the concepts of Neuro-

Linguistic Programming (NLP) and also leans heavily on the work of Milton Erickson. The latter was studied by the developers of NLP, who described their findings in the books *Patterns of the Hypnotic Techniques of Milton H. Erickson, Volume 1* (Bandler & Grinder, 1975) and *Volume 2* (Grinder, DeLozier, & Bandler, 1977). *A Teaching Seminar with Milton H. Erickson* (Zeig, 1980), edited with commentary by Jeffrey Zeig, is a record of a week-long seminar given by Erickson shortly before his death. Erickson did much of his teaching by means of stories and the book contains many examples of his use of metaphor.

Also heavily influenced by NLP and Erickson's work was David Gordon whose book *Therapeutic Metaphors* (1978) described in detail how a large scale metaphorical scenario might be developed for a particular clinical situation.

Oriental Stories as Tools in Psychotherapy (Peseschkian, 1986), originally published in the United States in 1982 with the title *The Merchant and the Parrot*, offers us many stories with therapeutic potential from different Eastern cultures.

Stories for the Third Ear: Using Hypnotic Fables in Psychology (Wallas, 1985), describes a variety of psychotherapeutic challenges, each followed by a story the author used to help the client. In each case, there then follows a brief account of changes noted after the telling of the story.

My Voice Will Go With You: The Teaching Tales of Milton H. Erickson, M.D. (Rosen, 1982) consists of a series of stories and anecdotes, many quite short, used by Erickson, with commentary by the editor of the book. There is great clinical wisdom in this book.

Doris Brett's *Annie Stories* (1988) contains ideas for stories parents might read to their children in various situations. They deal with such matters as fears, the arrival of a new baby in the family, divorce, and dealing with such stresses as death, pain, and going to the hospital. While this book and its successor, *More Annie Stories* (Brett, 1992), are addressed to parents rather than therapists, they con-

tain interesting ideas for the construction of therapeutic
stories.

Many sources are available for the student who wishes
to explore the rich heritage of fairy tales. *The Reader's
Digest* published two volumes entitled *The World's Best
Fairy Tales* (Sideman, 1967). Many fairy tales were collected by Andrew Lang, who published a whole series of
fairy tales, including *Blue Fairy Book* (1889, 1965), *Red
Fairy Book* (1890, 1978), *Green Fairy Book* (1892, 1978),
Crimson Fairy Book (1903, 1951), *Brown Fairy Book*
(1904, 1965), and *Lilac Fairy Book* (1910, 1968). In *The
Rainbow Fairy Book* (Hague, 1993), Michael Hague has
selected and illustrated some of the best of the fairy tales
from Lang's books—to make a volume well worth looking
through whether or not you are interested in constructing
therapeutic metaphors.

SUMMARY

Metaphor is the use of one thing to represent another.
Novels, short stories, anecdotes, fairy tales, tasks, rituals,
drawings, paintings, sculptures, and other artistic productions can—and often do—carry meaning metaphorically.
Metaphors may be more effective than straightforward,
direct methods of communication. This applies as much to
that form of communication we call psychotherapy as it
does to the many other situations in which metaphors can
be used, but they are only one of many strategies that are
used to make our communications more effective. Metaphor can be used to assist in the development of rapport
with our clients; it can help in the establishment of treatment goals; and it has many uses in the course of treatment,
once goals have been established. There is extensive literature on the subject of therapeutic metaphors, which have
an established place in psychotherapy.

3

THE TYPES OF METAPHOR

Have you ever been surprised to discover how much you know? I know I have. I am the host of a jazz program that is broadcast each week on a local radio station. Usually I prepare carefully what I am going to say. If the program is to be about a particular musician, band, or topic in jazz, I read as much background material as I can, assemble in my mind, and then in a script, the points I want to make, and proceed to select the appropriate music to go with the material I have.

One day I was caught quite unprepared. Only minutes before the broadcast, I was offered the opportunity to interview a well-known jazz musician who was playing that night in a club in the city. I knew of this man, of course, but I had done no reading or research on him and at first my mind seemed blank. I was aware that he was a saxophonist, but at that moment, as I was being asked to interview him, I could think of little else about him.

Soon the two of us were seated comfortably in the studio in front of our microphones. The familiar opening music— the theme I use every week to introduce the broadcast— was playing...and then the moment came for me to introduce my guest and start the interview with him. To my surprise, I found I had no difficulty at all. The questions came freely, they seemed appropriate, and as subject after subject came up, the required information seemed to come to me.

*Everything I needed to know must have been there,
somewhere in my mind, all the time! I just didn't know that
I knew!*

EIGHT TYPES OF METAPHORS

Almost any type of metaphor may be used in the course
of psychotherapy, and almost anything has the potential to
be used as a metaphor for something else. For the purposes
of discussion, however, it is convenient to divide metaphors into the following categories: 1) major stories;
2) anecdotes and short stories; 3) analogies, similes, and
brief metaphorical statements; 4) relationship metaphors;
5) tasks and rituals; 6) metaphorical objects; 7) artistic
metaphors; and 8) cartoon therapy. These are discussed
below.

1. Major stories

These are carefully constructed, often quite long, stories
tailored to the perceived needs of particular clinical situations. They are intended to deal comprehensively with
clinical problems. They are, perhaps, what the Book of Job
is to the parables of Jesus Christ. Gordon's (1978) book is
concerned primarily with the details of how such metaphors may be constructed. Although they are listed first,
major stories are one of the most complex forms of therapeutic metaphor. Therapists approaching the task of learning to use metaphors in treatment should probably not
attempt to use them until they are familiar with other
metaphorical methods.

Major stories are discussed further in Chapter 7.

2. Anecdotes and short stories

These have limited goals and aim to make specific
points in a concise and focused way. The story at the

beginning of this chapter carries several messages—or at least there are several messages which the listener may hear, unconsciously if not consciously. The most obvious message is one that Erickson was often at pains to emphasize—we know more than we think we know. This was a major assumption underlying much of his work. Not only do we know a lot more than we are aware of at any particular time, but in addition we do not know what we know. It is an everyday experience for most of us that we are often unable to call to mind information we feel we should be able to recall. There is something there, but we can't bring it to mind. We may feel that it is "at the back of our mind," but it is, for the moment, out of our reach. Yet, given the right situation, names, memories, and ideas sometimes flash back into our consciousness rather as a meteorite suddenly appears and flashes across the night sky.

Does the anecdote at the start of this chapter carry any other meanings? There are probably several, but I will mention only two. I was "sitting comfortably in the studio," a familiar place for me since I used it every week. I was seated in front of the microphone I spoke into each week, listening to the music that I heard at the start of each broadcast. In other words, it was the comfortable, familiar surroundings associated with the task of broadcasting that helped me recall my unconscious store of information and enabled me to use my interview skills to accomplish the task at hand. There is a message here about state-dependent learning. Thus, the anecdote may suggest metaphorically that we may perform tasks more effectively in situations in which we have practiced or performed the task at hand on previous occasions.

Then there is the phrase, "The questions came freely...as subject after subject came up." To me, at least, that conjures up a picture of my unconscious mind feeding me information and ideas. It offers to the reader or, if it is spoken, the listener an image of ideas coming freely into a person's mind as they are needed.

It reminds me of the automatic, thermostatically controlled furnaces that heated the hop drying kilns on an English farm where I spent many of my summers as a child. The fuel, a coal product reduced to quite a fine consistency, was carried into the furnaces by a rotating screw. The system was controlled so that just the right amount of fuel was fed into the furnace when required, maintaining the temperature in the kiln in the proper range. At all times, the furnace received just the amount of fuel it needed.

The description of the feeding of the furnace mentioned above is, of course, another example of the use of a metaphor to make a point. Ideas often come just as they are needed, as fuel did to the furnace.

Here is another anecdote, which makes—or offers to the listener—another point:

A man rode his camel a great distance in order to listen to the teaching of the prophet Mohammed. Leaving his camel outside the house where Mohammed was teaching, he entered eagerly. He listened to the prophet all day, returning to where he had left his camel at sunset. Then, to his dismay, he found that his camel had wandered off and was nowhere to be seen. Feeling cheated, he returned to speak to the prophet.

"How could God allow this to happen when I was listening to you speaking of Him?" he said.

The prophet replied, "Trust God and tie up your camel securely."

3. Analogies, similes, and brief metaphorical statements

These are usually offered with aims similar to those in anecdotes. They are commonplace devices widely used in everyday conversation. They are in no way specific to psychotherapy, but they can sharpen up our communication and make points more tellingly. The phrase above about ideas flashing into one's consciousness "as a meteorite suddenly flashes across the night sky" is an example. Describing ideas coming to a person in that way may carry more force than simply saying, "Ideas kept coming into my mind."

During the time preceding the 1994 South African elections, Connie Mabuza, a black South African living in Soweto, was talking to a reporter (Monroe, 1994). Commenting on the violence that was occurring and was threatening to mar the elections, she said:

> We have learned to look at these events as the pain and the blood of a woman who is in labor and about to give birth to a beautiful, bouncing baby. It's worth it.

Proverbs also are age-old means of making points by using brief, pithy statements like, "A stitch in time saves nine," "Too many cooks spoil the broth," or "People in glass houses shouldn't throw stones."

Poetry uses metaphorical devices freely. Wordsworth, in *The Daffodils of Ullswater*, talks about wandering "lonely as a cloud," conjuring up, perhaps, the image of a lone cloud floating across a blue sky and making his point much more effectively than simply writing, "I felt lonely as I wandered."

4. Relationship metaphors

In these, one relationship is used as a metaphor for another one—often one that is in some trouble. Milton Erickson's advice that "If you want a man to tell you about his brother, tell him about yours" is an example of how we may use one relationship as a metaphor for another. Here is an example (Barker, 1985):

All five members of the Evans family had attended
the preceding four family therapy sessions. They
had originally sought help because John, 14 years
old, the oldest of the three children, had developed
some rather severe behavioral problems. John's
behavior had now improved and he was back in
school; the concern of the family had lessened
somewhat. Today, for the fifth session, the father
was absent.

The therapist's earlier assessment had suggested
that Mr. Evans had always been a somewhat periph-
eral figure within the family. He appeared to have
been rather uninvolved emotionally with the other
family members, busying himself with his work
and leaving the care of the children and the home to
his wife. When John developed his problems, the
father became temporarily more involved with the
family, but the therapist hypothesized that things
were now slipping back to their former pattern now
that John's behavior problems had lessened.

On discovering that Mr. Evans was not only
absent from this session but had also said that he felt
no need to attend further sessions, particularly
since he was very busy in his business, the therapist
decided to address the matter of the father's absence
at the start of the session. The question was how to
do this. It did not seem a good idea to criticize the
father, either explicitly or implicitly. Any such
criticism would have almost certainly have found
its way back to Mr. Evans by way of at least one of
the family members. It would be more likely to
increase his resistance to coming. Nor did it seem a
good idea to blame the other members of the family,
though the therapist did have the impression that
they did not show much warmth or caring for the
father. So the following approach was adopted.

As the session started, the therapist asked all the
four family members present, in turn, what they
thought the therapist might have done in the last

session, or during the preceding ones, that had contributed to Mr. Evans' absence today. Had he said something tactless to him? Had he made him feel left out of the discussion? Had he shown him insufficient care and concern? Not enough warmth and acceptance, perhaps? Did the father feel in some way blamed for the family's problems? How could the therapist have helped him feel more a part of the therapy process? How had the therapist apparently managed to leave Mr. Evans with the idea that treatment could proceed satisfactorily without him? What could the therapist do now that would help the father once again become part of the therapy process? (pp. 25–26)

While it was perfectly possible that the therapist might have done any or even all of the above things to put Mr. Evans off from attending therapy, each also had metaphorical potential. They offered to the family members present the possibility that they might have done some of these things. Each time a question was put to the family about what the therapist might have done or failed to do that could have contributed to the father's absence, each family member had the opportunity—in a sense, even the invitation—to consider what he or she might have done to discourage Mr. Evans from attending. At the same time, they were in no way being accused of doing any such thing; on the contrary, the therapist was suggesting that he may have been the person responsible.

The discussion of the possible reasons for the father's absence thus used the therapist's relationship with the father as a metaphor for the other family members' relationship with him. It was always possible that some or all of the family members might not take the questions in this way, even at an unconscious level, but in that case nothing would have been lost. Much might have been lost, however, in terms of the therapist's relationship and rapport with the family members, if he had even suggested that the family members were in some way responsible.

This is but one illustration of the point made in Chapter 2, that metaphors leave those to whom they are offered the choice of "buying into" them or not doing so. If the material offered proves not to have a metaphorical meaning for them, it is usually simply accepted at its face value and no harm is done—as would have probably been the case in this example, if these issues had been addressed directly. How much better than addressing these questions in ways that directly suggest blame or responsibility for the family members!

5. Tasks and rituals with metaphorical significance

Tasks, whether carried out once or repeated as rituals, can carry metaphorical meanings. All human societies seem to have rituals that have been developed to serve particular purposes. We have our weddings, funerals, baptisms, bar mitzvahs and other coming-of-age rituals, as well as ceremonies celebrating all kinds of events and marking various special occasions.

Religious ceremonies such as the celebration of Christmas or Ramadan carry deep meanings and come to have great significance in societies in which they are practiced. Thus Christmas, the origins of which probably stretch back even before the birth of Christ, has come to be "the season of goodwill." Its celebration may be seen as symbolizing our capacity to love one another, something of which we seemingly need to be reminded at least once a year. It is so powerful that wars are sometimes put "on hold" as Christmas truces or cease fires are declared.

A rich source of information on the use of rituals and tasks is *Rituals in Families and Family Therapy* (Imber-Black, Roberts, & Whiting, 1988). This book offers many examples of the roles of rituals in families.

Rituals often prove valuable in a wide variety of clinical situations, but are perhaps especially useful at transition points—the end of a phase in the life of an individual or family and the start of another, or the transition from one situation to another. They often can be used productively at the termination of therapy.

They will be discussed further, with examples, in Chapter 7.

6. Metaphorical objects

One object may be used in therapy to represent another. Play therapy with children makes much use of play materials and objects in metaphorical ways. Children can often express and deal with problems through the medium of play, used metaphorically, better than they can in direct conversation.

Objects with metaphorical meanings may be incorporated into rituals or they may play a part in other therapeutic strategies. For example, family secrets—subjects about which family members may find it difficult to talk openly—may be "sealed" in an envelope (which need not actually contain anything) and then be talked about without actually being named. The envelope then becomes a metaphor for the secret.

One of the most time-honored of metaphorical objects is the scapegoat. This goes back to biblical times. It is described in the Book of Leviticus (which, incidentally, is replete with descriptions of metaphorical tasks and objects). As Leviticus has it, a goat is selected to become the metaphorical object. Then Aaron, the priest, was "to put both of his hands on the goat's head and confess over it all the evils, sins and rebellions of the people of Israel, and so transfer them to the goat's head. Then the goat is to be driven off into the desert by a man appointed to do it. The goat will carry all their sins away with him into some uninhabited land" (*Good News Bible*, 1976).

In therapy today, the use of live animals as metaphorical objects is generally frowned upon, but the burying or burning of things that symbolize the end of a relationship or a phase in a person's or a family's life can serve similar purposes.

The "12-Step" program of Alcoholics Anonymous is of interest in this context. The fourth step reads, "We made a searching and fearless moral inventory of ourselves." It leads to Step Five, "We admitted to God, to ourselves, and to another human being the exact nature of our wrongs." As these steps are usually practiced, the person "working" them is advised to write down his or her "moral inventory," using guidelines of which there are several versions. Then, after completing the fifth step, and having shared the contents of the inventory with another person, the individual may tear up or burn the written material, symbolizing a letting go of the past and its "wrongs." This frees the recovering person to move ahead and reconstruct his or her life in the course of working the remaining seven steps.

7. Artistic metaphors

Many people can express their feelings and ideas better through such media as drawing, painting, and sculpture than by talking and writing. Art therapy is increasingly being used in the course of psychotherapy. These methods can be of particular value in work with children. Many books have been written on the interpretation of children's drawings (e.g., DiLeo, 1983).

While it is common knowledge that painters, sculptors and other artists have long used their various media to represent things in metaphorical fashion, Mills and Crowley (1986) have developed the use of such materials as therapeutic devices. They provide a detailed account, with examples, of how to use this valuable approach.

8. Cartoon therapy

This is another metaphorical approach described by Mills and Crowley (1986). It is quite closely related to therapy using artistic metaphors. It is, perhaps, a peculiarly American phenomenon, using, as it does the cartoons and their characters developed for movies and television by Walt Disney and others. In this age of television, cartoons with a vast range of characters and situations are presented in profusion on television at times when there is a large audience of children. Cartoons are also found in newspapers and in "comics." Many children readily identify with characters such as Superman, Batman, or the Power Rangers. Cartoons are familiar to them and represent "fun." The medium thus lends itself to use with children and can facilitate the indirect communication of ideas and feelings with those who are inclined to communicate in this way—as many children are.

Artistic metaphors and cartoon therapy are discussed further in Chapter 7.

REFRAMING AND METAPHORS

What do all the above metaphors have in common? They are all designed to change the meaning of something. This process is often referred to as "reframing." These metaphors offer different understandings of situations; of people's views of themselves or others; of relationships; of how problems may be solved; or of our past experiences; or of what the future may hold for us.

Some believe that the integration of "left brain" and "right brain" functions is one of the chief mechanisms whereby metaphors accomplish their therapeutic aims. Precisely what the neurological mechanisms are may be less important than the changes in function that occur. Indeed, the "left brain/right brain" concept is something of a metaphor in itself.

The clinically apparent fact is that we all seem to have two parts—a rational, logical, thinking mind and an emotional, often apparently irrational one. The latter can lead us to do great things, to write poetry, compose music, and come up with all kinds of creative ideas and productions. It can also be destructive when, despite the understandings of the "logical, rational" mind, we find ourselves thinking of or engaging in destructive or self-destructive activities.

While the neurological basis of all this is certainly of interest, for the practicing therapist the important thing is to develop skills in dealing with the dichotomy that appears to be within all of us.

SUMMARY

Various types of metaphor are available for use as tools in psychotherapy. They range from major stories to analogies and similes. One relationship can be a metaphor for another. Tasks, rituals, and objects can carry meaning metaphorically, as can artistic productions and cartoons.

Metaphors can have powerful effects in reframing situations, relationships, and other aspects of the human condition. It seems that they facilitate communication with that part of the mind—often associated with the right cerebral hemisphere—that is concerned with creativity, poetic ideas and intuition, rather than confronting the part that is concerned with rational, logical thought.

4

INDICATIONS FOR THE
USE OF METAPHORS

I once knew a very intelligent man whose only apparent problem was a high degree of obstinacy. He seemed to have strong, well developed, and, usually, logical ideas about how to do things. Probably, his ideas worked well in many situations, for he ran a successful business and was widely respected for his intellect. Many people came to him for advice.

Successful as he seemed to be in his business, John had decidedly less success as a parent. That was how I came to know him, for he came to me to discuss the problems he was having with his children. There were three children in the family, a teenage boy named Ken, and two younger girls. The boy was becoming rebellious, failing to come home from school on time while offering blatantly implausible explanations for his lateness, and showing a total disregard for the homework tasks set him at school. His sisters did not present problems as severe as Ken's but John felt that they were starting to follow in his footsteps.

John had what was to him a very logical approach to dealing with Ken's behavior—punish him. Ken was "grounded" for increasingly long periods of time. Other sanctions included loss of the use of the telephone, restrictions on the places John was allowed to visit and whom he was allowed to associate with, and reduction and finally discontinuance of his weekly allowance. Ken's behavioral problems did not lessen as the severity of the sanctions was progressively increased. If anything they got worse. Yet John continued to believe that the only logical response was to increase their severity further. It seemed he could not conceive that any alternative response was possible, despite the opinion expressed to him by others, including Ken's mother, that he needed to devise other ways of dealing with the problem.

How often it is that we get fixed in rigid patterns of behavior and seem to be unable to break out of them! This happens on a relatively small scale in many families, on a somewhat larger scale in, for example, industrial confrontations, such as union/management disputes, and on a scale that is larger still in some political confrontations. Examples of the latter, as this is written, include the Northern Ireland conflict; the war in Bosnia; and the inter-tribal slaughter in Rwanda. There are many others and more will have developed by the time this appears in print.

The "cold war" between the "democracies," led by the United States, and the "communist" bloc, led by the former USSR, was such an example on a vast scale, with the two sides arming themselves with escalating arsenals of weapons of mass destruction. In much the same way, the conflict between Ken and his father had escalated.

How can these situations be defused or, better still, resolved? The basis of virtually all of them is the clinging, by the protagonists, to beliefs or attitudes that make resolution of the problems impossible. In many cases an impartial consideration of the situation by an unbiased outsider reveals a lack of logic in the positions taken by the protagonists. To take the case of Ken and his father as an example, it was fairly clear to most of those involved, including Ken's mother, that the way the father was attempting to deal with his son's difficult behavior was ineffective. The two of them were engaged in an unproductive power struggle, each combatant hoping eventually to vanquish the other, even though there was nothing to suggest that victory was in sight for either side.

In such situations, both protagonists need new perspectives on what is happening; at the very least, one of them does. Otherwise the conflict is likely to escalate. Sometimes, physical violence, occasionally even murder, develops. Metaphor can help provide the new perspectives needed. The story at the beginning of this chapter could be either an actual clinical situation—and it is one I have encountered many times in my practice as a child and family psychiatrist—or it could be used as a metaphor for an analogous situation in a field other than father/son conflict. Situations are common in which people keep repeating, against all the evidence of their experience, attempted "solutions" to problems—but their solutions do not work. It's rather as if a man who is attempting to drive to a certain destination finds that the route he has taken does not lead to where he wants to go. Being at a loss to know what road to take, he decides to return to his starting point. Then, he sets out once more but, inexplicably, takes the same road as before and finds himself in the same location where he got lost previously. It would be even more surprising if he tried the same route yet again...and again... and again.... Yet, that is what we sometimes see happening in families in conflict, and in other situations.

So metaphor is a way of offering new choices and new perspectives. These can lead to the resolution of conflict and the solution of many other problems.

The story about the driver taking the wrong route is one which I have used from time to time in attempting to offer new choices to people in difficulties of one sort or another. And, as we have seen in Chapter 2, there are other strategic devices available that may achieve similar objectives.

A TWO-STAGE APPROACH

There are two questions that need to be asked when we must decide whether or not to employ metaphor as a major therapeutic maneuver. They are:

1. Is a strategic approach required?
2. If the answer to question 1 is yes, then is metaphor the appropriate, or the best, strategy to use?

1. Is a strategic approach indicated?

What we are considering here is whether a "frontal assault" on the problem is the best plan, or whether a less direct one is indicated.

"Strategic therapy" is usually defined as therapy that uses a plan, which may be complex, to produce change, as opposed to offering a simple directive or a task that is mutually agreed as offering a straightforward solution to the problem. Cloe Madanes (1981) puts it in these words: "The responsibility is on the therapist to plan a strategy for solving the client's problems" (p. 19). What is less clear is how complex a therapy plan has to be for it to be deemed "strategic." In a sense, all therapy is, or should be, strategic, for the therapist must have a plan of some sort—a scheme in his or her mind even if it is not committed to paper or formulated in detail. And even a frontal assault needs planning!

I prefer not to use the term "strategic" in relation to psychotherapy. I believe a better distinction is that between "direct" and "indirect" methods of therapy. Using the example of the case described at the beginning of this chapter, a direct approach would be to say to the father something along the following lines:

> It seems as if you've tried very hard to deal with your son's behavior problems by using punishments of various sorts. It's obviously been disappointing to you that none of the punishments you have tried has worked. Perhaps it's time you tried another approach. What about our helping you develop a plan for encouraging the behavior you want to promote, rather than just punishing Ken for his misdeeds? Or maybe we should get your wife and Ken together—and maybe have the two girls join us as well, to see if we can work out a new plan of action?

This sort of approach—logical and rational—may be successful. It often is. Sometimes, however, our clients are either unwilling to take a different approach for any of a whole range of reasons; such as: preconceived ideas that fly in the face of what we are suggesting; a firmly held belief in punishment; reluctance to examine the nature of the communication in the family; or disagreement between the parents on what approach to take.

Another possibility is that the family does agree to what is suggested, tries it, and finds that it does not achieve the desired aims. This can happen for several reasons—perhaps because the family does not carry out the tasks, or make the changes suggested, in a consistent and persistent way; or because the suggested approach, though implemented, has overlooked some aspects of the problem or proves to be deficient in some other way.

Sometimes individual clients or families have had much previous therapy that has failed to resolve their problems. In such cases it is always important to explore carefully what has been tried. If it proves that a series of direct injunctions and logically explained and rational treatment plans have failed, it may be better not to try more of the same. It may be preferable to devise an indirect approach without trying a direct one first.

2. If an indirect approach is indicated, what sort of indirect strategy should be used?

A list, by no means exhaustive, of available indirect approaches, was set out in Chapter 2. How, then, do we set about deciding which one to use?

There are few hard data to tell us which of the many possible indirect ways of conveying therapeutic messages should be used in any particular clinical situation. In practice, much seems to depend on the preference and experience of the therapist. This is not necessarily bad. Psychotherapy is as much art as science, and we all have our personality characteristics and preferred ways of working. Some of us are accomplished storytellers; others have a dramatic flair and take readily to the use of psychodrama and the acting out of family conflicts in family sculpting;

others have a ready wit which they find they can use as a powerful therapeutic tool; yet others find themselves to be quite at home devising and delivering paradoxical directives. By all means, therefore, capitalize on the resources within your own personality and those provided to you through experiences in other areas of your life.

While you are certainly likely to be more successful using therapeutic techniques with which you are familiar, it is important also to have a large therapeutic armamentarium. The techniques with which you feel most comfortable, and which come most naturally to you, will not prove effective in every case. Some clients are unmoved by family sculpting, while others fail completely to respond to the use of humor. So the choice of indirect strategy cannot depend simply on the basis of the therapist's degree of comfort with different methods.

So, what are the clinical situations in which metaphorical methods are most likely to be desirable?

Children generally have a great love of stories. Many are read stories at home by their parents and almost all have this experience in school, especially in their early school years. As a result, most accept quite readily being told stories when they meet their therapist. Indeed, the telling of stories, which need not have any special metaphorical message, is often an excellent way of establishing rapport and helping children feel at home in the initially strange situation of the therapist's office or playroom. Stories may therefore be a prime medium for the conveying of messages to children, whether these are metaphors or messages of some other sort.

OTHER CONSIDERATIONS IN THE
USE OF METAPHORS

Here are some other considerations related to the use of therapeutic metaphors:

The type of therapy

While metaphors can be used in virtually any type of therapy, they have a bigger role in some types than in others. Metaphorical methods are more likely to be needed when the information to be imparted—or offered in metaphor form—is somewhat complex, and when the client(s) are more resistant to change, and when the role of the therapist is more active.

In *psychoanalysis*, in which the therapist's role is limited largely to listening, asking questions, and making comments, often of an interpretative nature, the uses of metaphor are probably quite limited.

Metaphor can have a limited but valuable place in *behavior therapy*. Although the process of discovering the contingencies controlling behavior and then modifying them—the essence of much behavior therapy—does not readily lend itself to the use of metaphors, these may be of value in exploring the aims of therapy and explaining how behavior therapy works. Behavior therapy is essentially a learning process and for those who approach it with an element of suspicion, explanations that use other, more familiar, learning processes may be helpful.

In both psychoanalysis and behavior therapy, as with other forms of therapy, metaphors may help motivate clients and sustain their interest.

Metaphorical methods come fully into their own in the course of treatments in which therapists play active roles, offer clients ideas, suggest how problems and other behaviors may be reframed, provide clients with possible solutions to problems for them to consider, and even give instructions. It is in those types of therapy, usually termed "*systemic*" or "*strategic*," that they may be most used.

It may not be strictly correct to call *hypnotherapy* a treatment method in its own right, since the act of inducing hypnotic trance is in itself of limited therapeutic value. It is what happens once the subject is in trance that is of

importance. Here is where metaphorical methods really
come to their own. Hypnosis, perhaps by shutting down
"left brain" activity, seems to reduce people's critical
faculties, or at least those requiring logical, rational thought.
New ideas are often more readily accepted and incorporated into subjects' mental schemata during states of trance.
Moreover, the very process of focusing one's attention on a
story—or a movie, television show, or book, for that matter—
often induces a light trance state. One is temporarily
removed from the real world around one into that of the movie, the book, or whatever may be the focus of one's attention.

The clinical situation

We have seen that metaphor is often of value in situations in which direct communication has proved ineffective. Discussing the work of Milton Erickson, Zeig (1980)
has pointed out that the more his patients resisted his ideas
the more indirect and anecdotal Erickson became.

The following are some clinical situations in which
metaphor may be helpful.

"It's hopeless. I'll never make it."

Those who are pessimistic and dispirited can be difficult to help. Very often, direct reassurance is ineffective. It
is reasonable, indeed important, to say to the person who
expresses hopelessness that you do not share that spirit of
hopelessness. Many times, though, this has little impact.
Tales of those who have felt that way but have found that
things have turned out better than they expected may be
helpful. Despair turning to delight is a common theme of
many stories. The Ugly Duckling was in despair because
he was so ugly, and so different from his brothers and
sisters. (How often have our clients felt that way!) Things
seemed pretty hopeless for him. He felt destined to lead a
life of rejection and misery until—suddenly—he found he
was a beautiful swan! This was something he could not

have expected, yet it happened. In the twinkling of an eye his life was transformed!

The Ugly Duckling appeals to many children and also to many adults, but not all adults take kindly, and respond, to fairy tales. Metaphors must be selected to suit the interests and values of those to whom they are offered. For a person with a keen interest in the Bible, the story of the journey the people of Israel made through the wilderness to the promised land might have much meaning. The Israelites despaired and complained bitterly to Moses that he had led them to this desolate place where they felt they were going to perish. Yet Yahweh, their God, came to their rescue and eventually they did reach the promised land.

While I do not advise that you set yourself up as God, the metaphor of the journey from Egypt to the promised land has a certain resemblance to the journey our clients make in therapy.

History, past and present, is full of sudden breakthroughs: Columbus sighting land when his crew was beginning to despair; the sudden breaking down of the Berlin Wall; the collapse of the Communist regimes in Eastern Europe, and so on. Any one of these, or personal experiences of the therapist or others known to those involved in the treatment process, may be used in similar ways.

"I don't agree with you. Children need their parents to take care of them."

Sometimes our clients reject the advice given them by professionals from whom they seek help. The words above might be those of an overprotective parent who, for whatever reason, is reluctant to "let go" of a child. This can delay a child's emotional development. You may find that direct advice and instructions, however persuasively argued, fail to bring about change. A metaphor, perhaps in the form of a story, may be more helpful. With overprotective parents, I have often found the story of the Philippine Eagle useful.

The Philippine Eagle lays only one egg each breeding season. The mother eagle looks after her eaglet with great care, feeding it regularly until it is strong enough to fend for itself.

The big problem the mother faces as the eaglet grows up is that of knowing when the young bird can indeed take care of itself. If she allows it to leave the eyrie before it can make a kill for food or defend itself, it will perish, either from starvation or as a result of attack by another predator. If she waits too long, the best time for learning to make a kill will have passed. So the process of handing over responsibility to the young bird, and of teaching it to survive in the world, is a delicate one.

In practice, eagles usually survive. The delicate adjustment of roles occurs at just the right speed to give the young bird the best chance in life. The mother eagle watches carefully for all the signs that will tell her that the young bird has developed sufficiently to be allowed out of the eyrie. Perhaps the eaglet also has a feeling that tells it when it's strong enough to fend for itself. We don't know precisely how the process occurs. Probably instinct has a lot to do with it. And we can only wonder about the heart searching that perhaps goes on within both mother and her eaglet while we admire the way, time and again, they make the right judgments and the species survives.

"How could you suggest that?!"

Some ideas or concepts presented directly may upset clients. An example is the case of the absent father, mentioned in Chapter 3. To have suggested to the family members present that they had played a part in discouraging the father from attending might have upset them, or provoked cries of outrage or indignation. Offering them the idea metaphorically not only gave them or, perhaps, their "unconscious" or "right brain" the opportunity to consider the point, while accusing them of nothing. And, as with all messages delivered metaphorically, it also allowed them the possibility of rejecting the idea or not considering it at all.

"This is boring!"

While adults do not usually come out in such a forthright way and say they are bored during therapy, children tend to be freer in expressing how they feel. And adults, while they may not often say they are bored, nevertheless may be. It is usually easier to keep children involved and interested when they are seen on their own, especially if it is in a playroom, than when they are part of a session with their family. If the session is mostly talk, they may have difficulty following the conversation. Enlivening the session by means of stories, games, and activities, which can be devised so that they carry metaphorical meanings, may serve both to relieve or prevent boredom and to convey messages.

"You may...wish...to allow yourself...to be...transported...to a very special, safe, and comfortable place..."

Metaphors can be valuable during what is often known as the "utilization" phase of hypnotherapy. This is the phase that follows the induction of trance. Subjects in trance seem to be especially open to receiving messages presented when they are in the trance state. Lankton and Lankton (1983) suggest that the use of multiple metaphors during hypnotherapy can be a powerful way of enabling clients to make use of resources available in their unconscious. By presenting a series of metaphors, one offers subjects a lot of choice at the unconscious level (see Chapter 8).

Therapists' preferences

Storytelling, like using other metaphorical ways of communicating, comes more easily to some than to others.

So don't start until you are ready. It is important to be confident and at ease when using these or any other communication techniques. It is a wise plan to take as much time as you need in preparing your metaphor, so that when you do start to deliver it you are both ready and confident in what you are about to do.

There is much to be said for practicing storytelling before making use of it as a clinical tool for specific purposes. I have found, also, that it is helpful to make the therapy setting one in which clients become used to being told anecdotes and stories. Every anecdote need not be a metaphor designed to achieve a particular therapeutic end. Some may simply lighten up the conversation and contribute to the development of rapport. One snowy winter day a mother and her two children arrived quite late for an appointment with me. She apologized for her lateness, explaining that she was held up by a traffic accident involving several cars that had collided on the slippery roads. In the light of the circumstances she described, it seemed that she had done rather well to get to my office at all. I responded by telling her of a similar experience I had had the previous winter—an experience that had led me to be even later for an appointment than she was. This was intended to act both as an indication of my acceptance of the mother's lateness and as an expression of my appreciation that, though late, she had managed to get to the appointment as soon as she possibly could.

The telling of stories such as the above can have other uses:

(a) It can get clients used to the idea that stories will be told during therapy sessions. It defines them as a "normal" part of what will happen. It is not a good idea to wait until you have devised a carefully planned story, anecdote, ritual, or task, designed to achieve a particular metaphorical therapeutic function, before your clients have become accustomed to them being part of what goes on during therapy. Once clients have become accustomed to such activities, they are likely to take to them more easily and you will get a more ready response.

(b) It can model a useful style of communication. This may be valuable during family therapy, group therapy, or any therapeutic situation in which more than one client is present. The mere telling of stories, especially stories addressed to children in family sessions, offers a model of an effective way of communicating with children. Not all parents are in the habit of telling their children stories. Some may not have been told stories by *their* parents when they were children and this activity may not be part of their model of what parenting involves. Thus, if you tell children stories in their parents' presence, you are suggesting a communication technique that the parents may choose to adopt.

This is actually a relationship metaphor. You are offering to the parents the metaphor of your "storytelling relationship" with their children. If it proves effective, perhaps by grabbing the children's attention or by putting a point over effectively, the parents may, perhaps more unconsciously than consciously, adopt it as something they can use themselves. This may be more effective than simply telling the parents to tell their children stories, especially if this is something with which they do not feel at ease.

SUMMARY

Metaphor is often effective when direct communication has proven ineffective in getting meaning across. It is one of a number of strategic techniques that may be of value when more straightforward communication techniques have failed.

Before deciding to use a metaphorical approach, however, it is first necessary to decide whether an indirect—or "strategic"—approach is indicated and whether metaphor is more appropriate than a "frontal assault," which may have been attempted and failed.

Stories and play are particularly appropriate for use with children, but metaphor can be used in any age group.

The individual client's openness to the metaphorical medium and the therapist's degree of comfort with it are other relevant factors. Careful preparation is important and clients should be prepared for therapeutic metaphors by previously being offered communication using the medium concerned, be it a major story, an anecdote, a task, or some other device.

5

BASIC PRINCIPLES OF THE CONSTRUCTION OF METAPHORS

Have you ever thought about what a wonderful thing a fax machine is? You feed a document, a letter perhaps, or a report, or a certificate, or a timetable—even a picture—into a fax machine, then you dial a telephone number and press a button that tells the machine to scan the document, or the picture, and send a signal through the telephone lines to the destination you have chosen.

The machine at the other end may be just round the corner or a great distance away, even the other side of the globe. But, wherever it is, it can receive the signals coming in and convert them into a replica of what was sent. But have you noticed that the document that is printed out is not quite the same as the one that was sent? It is not as clear. The letters are not as sharp, the pictures lack some of their original detail. If the original had a variety of colors, they are not reproduced. Well, maybe there are color fax machines, though I have never heard about them. But even if there were, I doubt if they would reproduce the colors absolutely accurately.

The interesting thing about all this—to me—is that, even though they are sometimes a bit fuzzy and even faint, fax messages usually do convey the messages that are sent—unless there is something very wrong with the functioning of one of the machines involved. Originals in color, even when reproduced by fax in black and white, can still carry messages similar to those they originally had.

I have a friend who sometimes sends me faxes. He doesn't usually send me a written document; he usually draws a cartoon, either without any words on it at all or perhaps with just a few in "bubbles" coming out of the mouths of one or more of the figures in the cartoon. It can be quite a challenge to discover what the message is that my friend is sending, especially if it is only a picture—no words. Sometimes, it only hits me later. Sometimes I'm never sure I've properly understood what he is trying to tell me.

What might the above ramblings convey? Is there some possible metaphorical meaning to them? Could there ever be a place for them in a therapy context? When might one use the above material, or something like it, as a therapeutic tool?

MATCHING PEOPLE'S LANGUAGE

In Chapter 4 we saw, in a general way, how the use of metaphors may be of help during therapy and considered indications for their use. Before we discuss how to decide what kinds of metaphor to use in particular situations and with particular clients, we should consider how to decide upon the language to use in delivering the metaphor. This issue is discussed later in this chapter in the section headed, "Communication Styles."

Not only must we consider the language we should use but we need also to decide what metaphors to use in particular clinical situations, and how to present them. Might there be clinical circumstances under which the vignette above could be useful? Almost anything can be used as a metaphor, so the answer is almost certainly, "yes." More important is the question of when it might be used.

Communication by fax could be used as a metaphor for

communication in a family, or in other groups of people, as we shall see later in this chapter.

But why use a fax transmission as a metaphor? Deciding what metaphor to use is a matter of clinical judgment. One probably would not talk about fax machines with most children, though it is possible to conceive of exceptions to such an exclusion. Some children are remarkably knowledgeable about modern technological devices. Many people nowadays work at home and have their offices in their homes, equipped with computers, fax machines, and other sophisticated machines. So, some children become quite familiar with all this. In the movie *Sleepless in Seattle*, there appears a precocious little girl, the daughter of a travel agent who worked out of her home. Using the computer in her mother's office, the child was able to book an airline ticket for her friend, the little boy who wanted to fly to New York. For her, the fax metaphor would surely have been fine!

COMMUNICATION STYLES

It is important to note carefully the communication styles and metaphors used by the people with whom you are working. Much has been written, especially by the developers of "Neuro-Linguistic Programming" (NLP), about the different types of language people use. The developers of NLP studied carefully the work of some highly effective communicators, especially Milton Erickson, and it was from what they discovered in the course of their studies that they set forth the communication system to which they gave that name. They described what they discovered about Erickson's way of communicating in *Patterns of the Hypnotic Techniques of Milton H. Erickson, Volume 1* (Bandler & Grinder, 1975a) and *Volume 2* (Grinder, DeLozier, & Bandler, 1977). Subsequent publications defined and explained how to use NLP techniques (Dilts et al., 1980; Bandler & Grinder, 1979, 1982; Grinder & Bandler, 1981).

It was perhaps unfortunate that, rather than publishing their findings in professional journals and thus subjecting them to the rigors of peer review, the developers of NLP opted to present their findings in books. Moreover, these books were published mainly by publishing companies they were instrumental in setting up, rather than by established publishers.

Presumably because of the dramatic effects they claimed for their methods—effects that their techniques can indeed have—they also frequently used the term "magic" in the titles of their publications, for example in the two volumes entitled *The Structure of Magic, Volume 1* (Bandler & Grinder, 1975b); *Volume 2* (Grinder & Bandler, 1976); *Practical Magic: A Translation of Basic Neuro-Linguistic Programming into Clinical Psychotherapy* (Lankton, 1980); and *Magic in Action* (Bandler, 1984). It might be argued that the term "magic" has a more appropriate place in fairy tales than in scientific literature.

The above circumstances have, in some circles at least, cast something of a cloud over NLP. Nevertheless many therapists find its concepts useful. Mills and Crowley (1986), for example, set great store by several of its principles and techniques, and emphasize the importance of "learning the language of the child." And it surely is important to learn, or at least observe and temporarily adopt, the language of one's clients if one is to work effectively with them.

One of the central themes of Neuro-Linguistic Programming is concerned with the language styles and preferences of people. The term "representational systems" is used by the authors writing about NLP. By this, they refer to the type of material people tend to use to process information. Some language styles are more meaningful to certain people than to others. The three main "representational systems" are the visual, the auditory, and the kinesthetic. Some of us prefer to process information predominantly using the visual sensory channel; others prefer the auditory; and yet others the kinesthetic—which is perhaps better described using the less jargonistic term "feeling."

There are two other sensory channels—smell (or olfactory) and taste (or gustatory) but these are seldom, if ever, the preferred channel.

All of us use all of these representational systems—more simply referred to as sensory channels—from time to time, but most tend to favor one of them. The thesis that the developers of NLP have proposed is that each of us has a preferred sensory channel—one that we prefer to use when processing information that comes to our attention. Once it is clear which is the client's preferred channel, the therapist can use it to communicate more effectively.

How is one to determine which is a person's preferred language? The simplest way is just to listen to the person when he or she talks. The words to listen most carefully for are the predicates. These are words that say something descriptive about the subject of a sentence. They include verbs, adjectives, and adverbs.

Here are some examples of phrases that use visual predicates:

That looks good to me.
I see what you mean.
Things seem brighter today.
I can see a cloud on the horizon.
I'm in one of my blackest moods today.
I just can't visualize that situation.
In my imagination he was standing right there beside you.
Let me show you what I've made.
There seems to be some light at the end of the tunnel.
My apartment overlooks the valley.

In the above phrases, words that suggest that the person using them may be a "visual thinker" are *looks, see, brighter, cloud..horizon, blackest, visualize, imagination, show, overlooks* and *light at the end of the tunnel.*

Here are some phrases in which the representational system is auditory:

I hear what you're saying.
That sounds pretty bad.

It was like music to my ears.
It seemed to awaken him like a clap of thunder.
I arrived to the sounds of rejoicing.
There was too much static for me to figure out what it was all about.
I felt I had to voice my opinion.
There was no opportunity for me to get any peace and quiet.
They seemed to be working in perfect harmony.

All these phrases seem designed to convey information using predominantly auditory terms. Key words that suggest this include *hear, sounds, music to my ears, clap of thunder, static, voice, quiet, harmony.* We would be reasonably justified in assuming that a person predominantly using such phrases is primarily an auditory processor.

The following are examples of the use of feeling or kinesthetic language:

That's a great weight off my shoulders.
I'm up against a lot of heavy problems just now.
That feels about right.
I'm comfortable with that plan.
I need to get a proper grasp on that concept.
He seems to be completely out of touch with what is going on around him.
It hit me like a ton of bricks.
She seems to be burdened down with worries.
How does that grab you?
The entire project seemed to be slipping out of my grasp.

In the above phrases, "kinesthetic" words include *weight, heavy, feels, comfortable, grasp, out of touch, ton of bricks, burdened down, grab* and *slipping out of my grasp.*

Here are some examples of "olfactory" language:

This smells fishy to me.
The detective was hot on the scent of the criminal.
The whole thing reeked of corruption.

Finally, here are some phrases using "gustatory" language:

It left a nasty taste in my mouth.
She was sweeter than honey.
I had to face the bitter truth.

People who use olfactory or gustatory sensory channels as their representational system of choice are rare in our society—if they exist. Nevertheless, it is worth taking note when people do use either of these systems, because it may be helpful to respond in similar language. This can promote rapport and align you with the unconscious processes taking place within the person. Communication may thus be facilitated.

The developers of NLP also recommend observation of subjects' eye movements. There is some dispute about the validity of this method of determining which representational system is being used, and there seem to be exceptions to the general rules. Nevertheless, some therapists find that observing their clients' eye movements alerts them to the way the clients are processing information. According to Dilts et al. (1980, p. 80), the correlations between eye movements and language processes (that is "representational systems") are as follows:

Eye Movements	Representational System
Up and to the left	Eidetic (remembered) imagery
Up and to the right	Constructed (imagined) imagery
Eyes defocused	Imagery
Down and to the left	Internal dialogue
To left or right, at level of gaze	Internal auditory
Down and to the right	Kinesthetic (body sensations)

The above movements are illustrated in Figure 5.1. They are said to apply specifically to right-handed individuals. I have found the observation of eye movements to be of limited value, but they are mentioned here since many

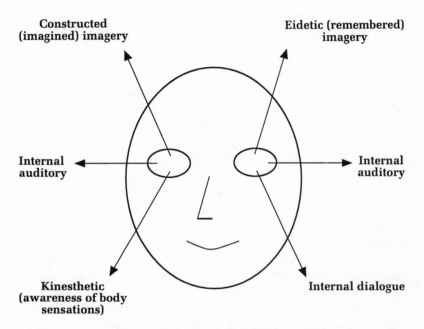

Figure 5.1. The suggested significance of eye movements.

therapists do find it useful. For further information about this, see Grinder, DeLozier, and Bandler (1977).

Mills and Crowley (1986) describe the "eye movement theory" with clarity, while acknowledging that its validity has not been scientifically proved. I have found that, for me at least, the most useful thing I can do is to pay careful attention not only to the predicates and the representational system they indicate, but also to all aspects of my clients' language. When you are dealing with children, it is essential, if you are to communicate effectively, to match the language you use to the language, including the vocabulary, sentence structure and complexity, and phrasing of each child. This applies whether or not you are using metaphors. It applies also to adults, whose levels of verbal sophistication vary widely. The language to use when speaking to a university professor is obviously going to be different from that which would be appropriate in conversation with a worker without a high school education.

CHOOSING METAPHORS

Now that we have some idea of how to determine the language to use, we are ready to consider how to decide on the actual metaphor.

Let us now consider the fax account at the start of this chapter. It is scarcely a story, more a series of reflections or musings. (Such musings, incidentally, seem often to be quite effective when offered to subjects in hypnotic trance, when their relevance is seldom questioned.) How could such musings be used for therapeutic purposes?

It is not too difficult to discern some possible metaphorical meanings. Communication by fax might be used as a metaphor for communication between people in a family or in some other context. So the "musings" might be used as a metaphor, or series of metaphors, about how people may communicate with each other in everyday life. A fax message corresponds fairly closely to the original message, but it is not as clear, colors are lost, and even shadings becomes less marked. But the message in a letter transmitted by fax can usually be accurately read and understood. If it is too distorted, though, its meaning may be lost partially or completely.

If there is color in the original, it is lost, to be replaced, perhaps, by various shades of gray. Nevertheless its subject and message may still be discernible. If a cartoon with little or no text is sent by fax, its meaning or message may not have been very clear before it was sent, and it may be less so after it has been transmitted and received. On the other hand, the very vagueness and ambiguity of the message may allow the person receiving it to use it in an idiosyncratic way that suits that person's particular needs at the time. Lack of clarity is not always a bad thing—witness the value of projective tests such as the Rorschach.

Consider how the various elements in the material above might correspond to features of real-life communication. We may use the term "isomorphic" for elements that correspond between the metaphorical and the real-life scenarios:

Metaphor	Real-Life
Message received by fax	Statement made in conversation
The letters are not as clear	A little of the meaning is lost
The colors are not reproduced as in the original	The communication received is not as vivid as that sent
The messages intended to be conveyed by cartoons are not always clear	Some people use illustrations that others do not understand
Deciphering some faxes can be quite a challenge	We sometimes must work hard to understand what others mean when they talk to us

Metaphors, like fax messages, may closely resemble the subject to which they refer, or they may be well disguised; there is an infinite variety of possibilities in between.

The fax metaphor could be developed further. For example, one could talk about how some messages never reach their intended destination, perhaps because the wrong number has been dialed; or about how some arrive but are overlooked, either because the recipient fails to look properly to see if a fax has arrived (that is, the listener is not paying proper attention to the speaker) or because there are so many faxes arriving that this one is missed in the confusion (that is, there is too much going on, or too many people in the vicinity are talking, so that what the person is trying to say is lost in the hubbub).

Obviously, the "ramblings" could serve to convey messages about person-to-person (rather than fax machine-to-fax machine) communication. But when might you use them? This is where the art, as opposed to the science, of therapy comes in.

I do not know of any scientific way of determining which particular metaphor to use in which particular clinical situation. Here I will make a confession. When I was preparing to write my previous book on therapeutic metaphors, I spent several months writing down every metaphor, long or short, verbal or nonverbal, simple or complex, that I used. I ended up with a long list of metaphors, most of which—though not all—had proved to be of value in some clinical situation. Then, as I was writing the book I referred repeatedly to my list of metaphors to see which one might serve as an illustration of the points I wanted to take.

Many might say that I was going about the whole process of developing metaphors and writing a book about them in the wrong way. Surely we should start with the available theory and use it to construct the appropriate metaphor(s) for the clinical situations in which they are to be used. Then and only then, you might argue, should we proceed to offer the metaphors to our clients. What I did might seem like putting the cart before the horse. I am not sure whether this is a valid objection, however. In my experience, the clinical context often provides the metaphor. The reality is that we all use metaphors. They pop into our minds, often quite spontaneously and with little effort on our part.

I doubt if the idea of using the transmission of messages by fax would pop into my mind, or into the minds of most therapists, during an interview with, for example, a farm worker who has had no experience of modern offices and the equipment in them. Conversely, I might hesitate before using life on a farm as a metaphor during therapy with a banker. In many instances our clients offer us their own metaphors that we can pick up and use (Kopp, 1995).

It is thus important to have in mind the social, cultural, and vocational background of any person to whom you are going to offer a metaphorical message. If you do use a metaphor from an area of life with which your client is unfamiliar, you will probably need to explain something about the subject as you go along.

Real or Imagined?

Should we take the metaphorical material we use in therapy from real life, or should we use either preexisting

material, like fairy tales or science fiction, or ideas arising
from our own imagination or that of our clients?

Once again, there is little to go on in the way of hard data,
but it seems that either approach can be effective. As a
general rule, children are more inclined to engage in
fantasy and have less need for things to be literally true
than is the case with adults. As I write this, my four-year-
old is pushing a construction he has made with a few
pieces of large Lego blocks around the floor, while an-
nouncing that it is a "monster truck." I have to confess that
to me it bears little resemblance to a truck, monster or
otherwise, but to my son, "It's a monster truck" for the time
being. It, or something very like it, could readily become
a spaceship or an airplane—or just about anything to
which my son's imagination could stretch.

Adults, by and large, do not have imaginations that are
quite as flexible as those of most children. For some,
stories based on real-life situations may be more effective
than are purely fictional ones. Nevertheless, the notion
that ideas can be conveyed through fiction is not a strange
one to most adults; purely fictional scenarios are often
effective with clients of all ages.

More important than whether or not the metaphor
comes, or purports to come, from real life is whether its use
promotes the development of what Rossi (1985, p. 42) calls
a "shared phenomenological reality." He sees psychotherapy as a growth process and writes of the "expansion
of awareness" and the "creation of new identity." At the
start of his book *Dreams and the Growth of Personality*,
Rossi (1985) states:

> The natural awakening of the mind in youth and the
> progressive realization of our unique talents in
> maturity are now recognized as a general process of
> expanding awareness and personality development.
> In the ideal case this personality development cul-
> minates in peak experiences of self-actualization
> and cosmic consciousness. (p. 1)

It is probably little exaggeration to say that in therapy we join our clients, usually quite briefly, as they travel this journey towards "self-actualization and cosmic conscious-ness." The key term here is "join." In some way, we have to enter our clients' worlds, temporarily, to give them some new awareness.

Later in the same book, Rossi (1985) hypothesizes that:

> The creation of a shared phenomenological world in common is the emotional basis for expanding awareness and the transformation of states of being via contact between two personalities.
>
> Correspondingly we may also say that the so-called "resistance" in psychotherapy (when no growth is taking place) is a consequence of the inability of therapist and client to create a shared phenomenological world in common. (p. 48)

One of the best means of creating the "shared phenom-enological world" is by using our clients' own language and metaphors. We have seen above how we may facilitate the joining process by adopting the predicates and vocabu-lary of our clients, but we need also to listen for and pick up their own metaphors.

Certain tales, legends, and traditions, however, seem to have almost universal meaning. The idea that within each of us there are strengths, abilities, and potentials that are not currently evident is embedded in so much literary material and folklore. The brave little tailor vanquishes the giant; the Ugly Duckling turns into a swan; Dick Whittington, against all the odds, was three times Lord Mayor of London; and David slew Goliath. Indeed people can use their native resources to triumph over the most adverse of circumstances.

In making this particular point, it can be helpful to refer not just to mythical or fairy-tale characters such as the brave little tailor, or even to biblical characters of 2000 years or more ago, but to more recent figures who are plainly fact not fiction. In a previous book (Barker, 1985), I drew attention to the example of Louis Armstrong, who grew up in what were just about as unpropitious circumstances as one can find.

Armstrong was born and spent his early years in a shack in James Alley. This has been described as "the lowest negro slum in New Orleans . . . dingy and dangerous, the whole area [was] peopled with an abnormally high percentage of toughs, robbers and 'women walking the streets for tricks.'" By the age of 11, Armstrong was in an orphanage. Yet he rose to fame and has been called an "American genius" (Jones and Chilton, 1971).

Milton Erickson was a master at using what his patients brought to him. Many examples are to be found in his extensive writings. An oft-quoted case is that of the deluded mental hospital patient who thought he was Jesus Christ. Rather than argue with him about this, Erickson accepted the man as he found him and confirmed that he was on earth to serve people. As O'Hanlon and Hexum (1990) summarize it, Erickson then told the man:

> ...there was a task he could do to serve people. Since it was desirable for the doctors to play tennis during their recreation hours because they were using the muscles God gave them, could the man possibly help by smoothing the dirt on the tennis court? The man agreed and became an excellent tennis court keeper. After some time, MHE mentioned that he understood that the man was a carpenter (Jesus had been a carpenter). The man could only agree that he was. MHE told him that to serve mankind, he could use his carpentry skill to build some bookshelves for the psychology laboratory. The man became the psychology department handyman. (p. 291)

Some might characterize Erickson's approach with this man as manipulative, and in a sense it was. Yet it turned an unproductive, chronic psychiatric patient into a productive one and, perhaps, a happier one. His mental condition was not cured but a significant step in his rehabilitation was achieved.

SUMMARY

In designing and using metaphors in our work, we must become aware of, and take into account, the communication and language styles of our clients. The sensory channels through which they prefer to process information must be observed. We should then respond by using language that corresponds to theirs and employs the type of predicates and vocabulary they use.

The elements in our metaphors should be isomorphic with those in the real-life situation to which the metaphors are to be applied. In many instances the metaphors we use will arise naturally in the contexts of the conversations we are having with our clients and of the clinical situations.

Both real-life and fantasy or imagined material may be used as vehicles for metaphor. Children tend to be especially open to the use of fantasy and play.

6

BEFORE YOU START: THE PREREQUISITES

Peter was worried about his 12-year-old daughter, Sylvia. She had had repeated attacks of tonsillitis over the past several years. They had been accompanied by a high fever in addition to a very sore throat, and each time she had missed about a week of school. Sylvia's parents consulted their family doctor who recommended that they take Sylvia to an ear, nose, and throat specialist with a view to having her tonsils and adenoids removed.

Rachel, Peter's wife, accompanied Sylvia for the first visit to the specialist. The doctor examined Sylvia, ordered some blood tests, and took a throat swab. At that time Sylvia had recovered from her most recent throat infection and was apparently well.

When Peter and Sylvia arrived at the specialist's—we'll call him Dr. X—office on the return visit, they were ushered into his comfortably furnished consulting room and sat there waiting for the doctor to come in. After a few minutes, he strode into the room, looking neither at Sylvia nor at Peter, but at the medical chart he was carrying. Without a greeting of any sort, he announced, as if to thin air, "No evidence of infection. Throat swab clear."

Peter wondered how he was supposed to respond to this statement. It sounded as if Dr. X was suggesting that he might not be planning to remove Sylvia's tonsils. So he spoke up.

"Yes, Sylvia's fine just now, but she has had five really bad throat infections this winter. She's been quite ill and she's missing a lot of school. Our doctor feels she should have her tonsils removed. We've hesitated a long time before bringing her to see you, but we think our doctor is right."

"I need to have proof of these infections. When I looked at her throat there was no sign of tonsillitis. We can't just take everybody's tonsils out, you know."

"I know that, but our doctor has examined her during each of the attacks. I'm sure he can confirm for you that these were bad attacks of tonsillitis."

Peter and Dr. X were getting increasingly antagonistic. Each dug in his heels ever more firmly. Finally, after several more exchanges characterized by increasing irritation and anger in Peter, he said, "I think you're the rudest doctor I've ever met. I've decided that even if you wanted to take my daughter's tonsils out, I wouldn't let you now."

With that he left the room and the office.

Following this bad experience, the parents consulted their family doctor. He was a little surprised by what they told him, since Dr. X was reputed to be an excellent surgeon. But he agreed to refer Sylvia to another specialist—Dr. Y, as we'll call him.

Dr. Y, proved to be as different as chalk from cheese when compared with Dr. X. He was affable, courteous, relaxed, and friendly. He sat Sylvia and her parents down in comfortable chairs and exchanged a few pleasantries before coming to the subject of Sylvia's problems. By the time he did, all three family members felt quite at home.

"I see that your doctor thinks that this young lady needs to get rid of her tonsils and adenoids," Dr. Y said. "Tell me when she started having this trouble and what's been happening to her."

Dr. Y listened carefully to their story, asking for clarification from time to time, and checking out with Sylvia what her subjective experience had been. Then he said, "Let's have a look at her throat."

*Dr. Y carried out his examination in a respectful, busi-
nesslike way, at each point explaining to all three family
members what he was going to do. When he had finished,
he sat facing the family members in a chair similar to
theirs, also taking up a posture like that of the parents, who
were sitting close together.*

*By this time the family members were feeling entirely
comfortable with Dr. Y. He did agree to remove Sylvia's
tonsils and adenoids, but it is more than likely that the
rapport between him and the family was by this time so
good that the family would have accepted a recommendation to delay the procedure if he had explained his reasons
for that recommendation.*

This story is true. It might seem inconceivable that a
professional person could behave like Dr. X, but it does
happen. The experiences of Peter, Rachel, and Sylvia are
good illustrations of how to deal with people and how not
to. Of course, the removal of tonsils and adenoids is hardly
an example of strategic therapy. Nevertheless, the establishment of a good degree of rapport is important if you are
going to expect people to allow you to carry out surgical
procedures (or psychological ones) on them or their loved
ones. When one is using strategic therapy, such rapport is
essential. For the delivery of therapeutic metaphors, rapport is a basic prerequisite for which there can be no
substitute.

WHAT IS RAPPORT?

The existence of rapport implies that there is a sympa-
thetic relationship and a state of trust and understanding
between those involved. Both understanding and trust
grow as the relationship develops—assuming, that is, that
the relationship does develop in a positive fashion; rapport is not an all-or-nothing matter, but one of degree.

An important aspect of rapport seems to be the degree of
emotional involvement between the persons concerned.

This seems to be essential also for successful hypnotherapy. Erickson, Hershman, and Sector (1961), in their book on medical and dental hypnosis, describe rapport in the following terms:

> ...that peculiar relationship, existing between subject and operator wherein, since it [hypnosis] is a cooperative endeavor, the subject's attention is directed to the subject and the operator's attention is directed to the subject. Hence, the subject tends to pay no attention to externals or the environmental situation, to respond only to the person doing the hypnotizing. (p. 66)

Rapport, like a camel, is easier to recognize than it is to describe in words. Dilts et al. (1980), writing of what they call "pacing"—an important aspect of rapport building, as we shall see shortly—seek to explain at least some aspects of it:

> When you pace someone—by communicating from the context of their model of the world—you become synchronized with their own internal processes. It is, in one sense, an explicit means to "second guess" people or to "read their minds," because you know how they will respond to your communications. This kind of synchrony can serve to reduce resistance between you and the people with whom you are communicating. The strongest form of synchrony is the continuous presentation of your communications in sequences which perfectly parallel the unconscious processes of the person you are communicating with—such communication approaches the much desired goal of irresistibility. (pp. 116–117)

A comment on the phrase "the much desired goal of irresistibility" is in order. These authors were, of course, writing from the perspective of ethical health professionals. We should be aware, though, that these techniques can be used in other ways, for example, in selling things and in persuading people to join organizations of various kinds. The potential for their destructive as well as their constructive use certainly exists. It seems that it is by first establishing such intense rapport that their communications become "irresistible," that charismatic leaders persuade people to follow them. It is thus that tragic events occur such as the mass suicide of the Reverend Jim Jones' congregation in Guyana or the tragedy at the compound of David Koresh and his followers at Waco, Texas. Among the world's ultimate experts in the establishment of rapport are the great confidence tricksters. How else, other than in the context of intense rapport, could obvious swindles be sold to willing buyers?

Once rapport is well established, the therapist—or anyone else who has established it—can say just about anything, however outrageous, without causing offense to the subject. If the remark is one that could be considered offensive or insulting, it may be taken as a joke, or at least as something that is not intended to be taken seriously.

When rapport is very intense, the subject's critical faculties may seem to be blunted, so that whatever is said is interpreted in a positive light, whatever its literal meaning. Moreover, when a state of great rapport exists, metaphors may be accepted which in other circumstances would be rejected.

HOW DO WE ESTABLISH RAPPORT?

Rapport develops when the right conditions exist. The therapist's job is, therefore, to create those conditions. Many people do this in some measure, great or small, without ever having received special training in rapport development. It seems to come naturally to them. This may be partly because of their temperamental make-up, but it is probably due more to modeling. They have likely witnessed or experienced the use of the techniques we are about to consider during their formative years. Almost as if by instinct, they respond to others in an empathic way, automatically doing the things we are about to discuss. You, too, will soon start to do them automatically once you have had a little practice in their use.

Rapport-building techniques may be divided into *nonverbal* and *verbal* categories.

Nonverbal techniques

The various nonverbal ways of promoting rapport are probably the more powerful of these two categories. The late Thomas "Fats" Waller, on one of his recordings made in the 1930s, observed that, "Tain't what you say, it's the way that you say it." And therein lies a great truth.

Virtually any aspect of your nonverbal behavior (even during speech) may contribute to the development of rapport or, on the other hand, to its destruction. Here are some key nonverbal behaviors:

- Voice tone and volume
- Rate and pattern of speech
- Body posture
- Body movements
- Inclination of head
- Breathing patterns

It can be an instructive experience to observe people in public places such as restaurants or lounges, and to study their behavior. It is often quite easy to see whether people seated together are in rapport with each other or not. Intense involvement is shown by the way they look each other intently in the face, leaning forward and settling back in their chairs in synchrony with each other; perhaps picking up their glasses or cups at the same times; and generally matching each other's behaviors in ways of which they are probably quite unaware consciously. By contrast, there may be others who are sitting awkwardly, saying little, and apparently uninvolved with each other. Their postures differ and they are not moving in synchrony with each other.

Following is further discussion of the nonverbal techniques (behaviors) listed above:

Voice tone and volume

Matching, as far as you can comfortably do, the voice tone and volume of those with whom you are conversing helps promote rapport. Obviously there is a limit to how closely one can match others' voices. It is usually impossible for a man accurately to match a woman's voice, or vice versa, but volume and some aspects of tone can always be matched.

Rate and pattern of speech

Note and adopt both the rate at which the person you are interviewing speaks and the way that person puts words and phrases together. This does not mean imitating a stutter or other speech dysfluency, though it may be helpful to speak quite slowly when replying to a person who stutters, so that the overall rate of verbal communication is similar.

Body posture and movements

Adopting a similar body posture to that of the person with whom you are conversing assists in the development of rapport. If that person leans forward, you should lean forward also; then, when the person settles back in the chair, you should settle back. Movements of the arms and legs—such as crossing and uncrossing the legs—can similarly be mirrored. While getting in tune with your client by adopting similar postures and movements is important, it is equally important not to overdo it. We do not need to behave like zombies, slavishly imitating everything our clients do. But done subtly, with just some of the behaviors mirrored at any one time, this technique can be a powerful means of promoting rapport.

I am sometimes asked whether clients ever become aware that I am "copying" what they are doing. They have not—at least no one has ever commented on it. Moreover, what I am suggesting is not "copying," if by this is meant doing exactly what the other person does. For example, if the other person puts her left hand to her face, I might put either my left or my right hand to mine, and I probably would not adopt precisely the same posture. You will probably find, also, that after you have been consciously using these techniques for a time, they will come naturally to you; you will then find yourself employing them without conscious thought.

The inclination of the head

The tilt of the head is another behavior that can be mirrored to help in the rapport-building process. Most people move their head frequently while talking. The movements are usually quite small, but gently mirroring them with small movements of one's own seems to be a powerful rapport-building technique.

Breathing patterns

For most of the time, we are not conscious of our rate, depth, or pattern of breathing. Only if we get seriously out of breath, as during violent exercise, or have our attention drawn to it for some other reason do we become aware of our breathing pattern. Hypnotists have long been aware of the value of paying attention to breathing patterns in establishing rapport. During induction of trance, it is helpful to synchronize the phrases you speak with your subject's breathing pattern. In addition, if you breathe at a similar rate and depth, taking specially deep breaths when your companion does, this can be a powerful way of getting in tune with that person on an unconscious level.

Verbal techniques

We have seen, in Chapter 5, how it is important to match clients' language when constructing and delivering metaphors in the form of stories and anecdotes. Matching predicates and adopting similar language are important also, in the development of rapport. As the discussion in Chapter 5 has indicated, you should not reply with, "I *see* what you mean," if you have been asked, "Do you *hear* what I'm saying?" At least, you should not do so if you are seeking to establish rapport.

Since these verbal techniques have been described in Chapter 5, they will not be repeated here, but they are as important in the rapport-building stage as in the delivering of metaphors.

RAPPORT BUILDING AS A CONTINUOUS PROCESS

While rapport building is a major task to be accomplished during the early stages of any professional relationship, it should never stop as long as the relationship continues. Rapport can be destroyed just as it can be fostered. The principles and techniques discussed above need to be used continually as long as the professional contact continues.

Finally, on the subject of rapport, it is important to bear in mind that building rapport is not just a matter of using the techniques set out above. These are only techniques. The basic principles of treating our clients with respect; acknowledging by our attitudes and practice that we are there to provide services for which, directly or indirectly, they are paying; being courteous at all times; being sensitive to their reactions to the input we provide; and always being open to their feedback—these must never be forgotten or ignored if we are to be successful in helping people in overcoming their problems.

A SOUND FORMULATION: THE BASIS FOR THE THERAPY PLAN

As with most human endeavors, psychotherapy usually works out better the more carefully it is planned. And the development of a good plan presupposes a sound understanding of the problems to which it is to be addressed.

Detailed discussion of how to assess individuals and families, and of how to formulate the problems and challenges with which they come to us, is beyond the scope of this book. What does need emphasis is the importance of having the best possible understanding of the case of the individual, couple, or family you are planning to treat. Clinicians differ in how much background history they find it necessary to explore and clarify before developing a treatment plan. A basic minimum is an understanding of how the presenting problems have developed, what has been tried previously to resolve them, and how effective the various measures have been. Many clinicians like to obtain a more comprehensive account of the individual's or the family's general development and background, perhaps exploring the extended family circumstances quite fully.

Particularly important, in addition to any historical information, is the best possible understanding of the forces and factors that are maintaining the problems. There is a limit to what one can do about the past—though therapy is often undertaken to modify the effects of past experiences. Ultimately it is the forces and factors that are responsible for the continuance of the problems that therapy must address and modify in some way.

Outcome frames

The developers of Neuro-Linguistic Programming (NLP), referred to in the previous chapter, coined the useful term *outcome frame*. This is the response for which one person offering a communication to another is aiming. The NLP thesis (but one that is by no means unique to that theoretical system) is that "the meaning of a communication is the response it elicits."

Whenever we communicate with another person we are seeking some sort of response. Even if all we say is "Hi"— or if our behavior is a simple nonverbal gesture such as the wave of a hand or the wink of an eye—we are seeking or expecting some sort of response. It may simply be that we expect the other person to say "Hi," and perhaps smile or wink in response. Whatever it is, this is our outcome frame. It does not have to be consciously formulated; indeed in the great majority of social situations it is not.

In psychotherapy, however, planning and forethought are required. It may be that some experienced and highly skilled therapists do operate intuitively, being guided more by their unconscious than by conscious thought processes. The ability to do this, however, comes only after long years of training and practice. An appropriate metaphor might be that of learning to drive a car. At first, driving requires much conscious attention to the actions and responses required, but after years of experience, these seem to become virtually instinctive. The experienced driver will even cope with an emergency situation when there is not time to think out what to do.

In his later years, Milton Erickson often operated intuitively—or so it appeared—but study of his earlier work and writings shows that as a younger man he was most diligent and painstaking in studying the problems of his patients and in devising ways of helping them.

Psychotherapy consists of the exchange of communications between therapists and clients. The communications the therapist offers the client are intended to promote change. In deciding what communications to offer, therefore, we need a clear idea of the desired outcome—or "outcome frame."

Defining and agreeing on the desired outcome

Much psychotherapy—to say nothing of other human activities—fails because clear objectives have not been established. Indeed, without objectives there can be no way of determining whether therapy has met with success or failure.

It is desirable to set positive goals. Many people come to therapy with negative ones. They want to feel less depressed or anxious, or to eat less, or to stop smoking. Or they want their children to stop fighting with each other or their teenage daughter to stop refusing to eat everything they give her at meals. These are reasonable enough motives for seeking the help of a therapist, but they say nothing about what our clients *do* want. How do they want to feel once they stop feeling depressed? Are there still some situations where depressive feelings might be appropriate? What are their children to do if they are to cease fighting? What will replace smoking or overeating in their lives? And so on.

Focusing on how people coming for therapy would like things to be at the successful completion of therapy can be a salutary experience. I have found this sometimes to be the case, for example, when I meet married couples who are seeking help to improve their relationships. They usually have plenty of complaints about how things are between them, but when asked how they would like things to be, they are often a lot less specific. Some of them are, at least temporarily, lost for words. If and when they do find words, they are likely to frame the changes in negative terms: "I want her to stop doing . . ." Or "I wish he wouldn't spend so much time on..."

Asking each partner to prepare a description, preferably a written one, describing how he or she *would* like the marital relationship to be proves a more difficult task. When it is accomplished, what each partner has written often comes as a surprise to the other.

> Wayne was tired of and quite dissatisfied with the home computer he had purchased several years previously. He had been pleased with it when he first got it, finding that he could do all kinds of things—word processing, accounting, setting up and maintaining a database for his home business—

but now he felt the time had come to upgrade it. It seemed to be too slow; it didn't have enough memory for some new programs he would have liked to use; and the printer couldn't handle graphics.

Several of Wayne's friends had recently obtained computers that seemed to be able to do all sorts of wonderful things his could not do. Yes, it was certainly time to upgrade.

So Wayne went to a local computer shop and told the salesman that he wanted a better computer system. The salesman asked him what system he currently had. Wayne told him about it.

"Well, we can certainly help you improve on the system you've got," the salesman said. "What exactly do you want your system to do? What sort of programs do you want to run? What operating system would you prefer? Do you need color graphics?"...and so on.

Wayne was floored. All he really knew was that he wanted a better system, one that wasn't so slow and wouldn't prove unsuitable for some of the applications he had in mind.

The salesman was patient with him and pointed out that there were many computers and printers available at widely differing prices and that if he wanted to buy a system that would do what he needed, he should define precisely the tasks required of it. Otherwise he might find that he had paid more than he need have done, or alternatively that he had a system that would not meet his current and foreseeable needs. The salesman suggested that Wayne give the matter some thought, and then return with a list of what he wanted his new computer to do, both now and in the future.

Wayne did as the salesman suggested, returning to the store a few days later with a detailed list of the functions he would want his new computer to perform, now and in the next two or three years.

This list was, of course, Wayne's outcome frame. He constructed it by looking ahead, in his imagination, to how things would be in his home office once he had a computer that would serve all his present needs in a quick and easy fashion. He even took things a little further by allowing himself to project into the future.

The world is full of examples of projects embarked upon without clear objectives. It has been said that the recent United States military operation in Somalia lacked well defined objectives. Its name, "Operation Restore Hope," rather suggests that. Restoring hope, like having a happy marriage, is a great idea, but what does it mean in practical terms?

Stories such as the one about Wayne can be useful when you have clients who either do not have, or cannot see the point in developing a clearly defined outcome frame. Many of our clients are seeking different emotional states. They want to feel "happier" or "less depressed" or "on top of things." These are all very reasonable aims, but they are no more precise than Wayne's desire for "a better computer." Happiness, for example, means little as a goal in itself. It usually comes as a consequence of one's life situation. Thus, if we have satisfying family, work, leisure activities, and healthy relationships with others, a state of happiness is likely to be associated with them. These are the things to plan and work for, not the abstract concept of "happiness."

Once the desired state has been described, there are some other questions to be considered:

1. *May the "desired state" have any disadvantages?*
   Sometimes, problems in a family, while causes of concern, nevertheless seem to serve purposes. For example, children's behavior problems can serve the function of keeping the parents together and talking to each other. When the marital relationship is under strain, the one thing the couple may be able to agree about is how worrying, or objec-

tionable, their child's behavior is. Similarly, concern about their anorexic teenager may unite a couple, but what is to keep them together when the anorexia is resolved?

2. *What other consequences may follow once the changes the client seeks have been achieved?* An advantage of developing a clear picture of the outcome frame is that its drawbacks can become evident. Moving to a bigger house may seem like a good idea, but who is going to keep it clean? What will the property tax bill look like? Will it mean living farther from your place of work? If so, how will you cope with the longer commuting time?

3. *What has stopped those concerned from making the changes sought?* This is really another way of looking at question 2. Presumably, if the present situation has existed for a long time, it must have some advantages. Are you sure you want to lose these?

4. *Under what circumstances do you want the desired changes to occur?* All behaviors need to be considered in context. Honesty and truthfulness are generally to be desired, but if, in occupied Europe during World War II, the Gestapo had come to your door looking for Jews to send to concentrations camps, you might well have been justified in lying about the Jews hidden in your loft.

5. *How quickly do your clients want to change?* While sudden change is often desirable, it can be hard to cope with in some circumstances.

Intermediate goals

Some goals are best accomplished in stages, especially if the way to achieving them is not entirely clear.

In parts of Africa, the jungle is very thick. It can be hard, as you are traveling through it, to know what direction to take. The local people have a way of dealing with this, though. As they are traveling in jungle country, they make frequent stops at which they climb a tree. Once up the tree they have a panoramic view of the area. They look for the next landmark in their journey, get a sense of the direction to travel in order to reach it, stopping to climb another tree whenever they need to orientate themselves again.

The therapy plan

The plan should come before the metaphor. We have discussed the indications for the use of metaphors in Chapter 4. Metaphors provide an indirect, strategic way of putting ideas across. They can reframe problems and situations, suggest choices or possible solutions and indeed serve any of the purposes set out in Chapter 2.

Therapeutic metaphors will usually be employed after other more direct methods have been tried without success. The case formulation should be the basis for the plan. Metaphors may be employed to achieve intermediate goals as well as the final ones. They may also be employed to help in the setting of clearly defined objectives, to motivate clients, and to suggest that desired changes are indeed possible.

Chapter 7 will examine these processes in more depth.

SUMMARY

A first priority before using therapeutic metaphors must be the establishment of rapport, using both nonverbal and verbal techniques. Nonverbal techniques include matching voice tone and volume; the rate and pattern of speech; body posture and movements; inclination of head; and breathing pattern.

Verbal techniques include matching clients' predicates and vocabularies, also noting the sensory channels that clients prefer and using congruent language in conversation with them.

The therapy plan should be based on a sound formulation of the case and on agreed objectives. The "outcome frame"—a picture of the state desired by the client(s)—should be clearly defined. Its possible drawbacks as well as its advantages should be considered. Intermediate goals on the way to the final one may be set.

7

USING THE DIFFERENT TYPES OF METAPHOR

Once upon a time there lived in Japan a rat and his wife. They came of an old and noble race, and had one daughter, the loveliest girl in all the rat world. Her parents were very proud of her, and spared no pains to teach her all she ought to know. There was not another young lady in the whole town who was as clever as she was in gnawing through the hardest wood, or who could drop from such a height onto a bed, or run away so fast if anyone was heard coming. Great attention, too, was paid to her personal appearance, and her skin shone like satin, while her teeth were as white as pearls, and beautifully pointed.

Of course, with all these advantages, her parents expected her to make a brilliant marriage, and, as she grew up, they began to look round for a suitable husband.

But here a difficulty arose. The father was a rat from the tip of his nose to the end of his tail, outside as well as in, and desired that his daughter should wed among her own people. She had no lack of lovers, but her father's secret hopes rested on a fine young rat, with moustaches that almost swept the ground, whose family was still nobler and more ancient than his own. Unluckily, his wife had other views for her precious child. She was one of those people who always despise their own family and surroundings, and take pleasure in thinking that they themselves are made of finer material than the rest of the world. "My

daughter shall never marry a mere rat," she declared,
holding her head high. "With her beauty and talents, she
has a right to look for someone a little better than that."

So she talked, as mothers will, to anyone who would
listen to her. What the girl thought about the matter
nobody knew or cared—it was not the fashion in the rat
world.

Many were the quarrels that the old rat and his wife had
upon the subject, and sometimes on their faces were seen
certain marks that looked as if they had not kept to words
only.

"Reach up to the stars is my motto," cried the lady one
day, when she was in a greater passion than usual. "My
daughter's beauty places her higher than anything upon
earth," she cried; "and I am certainly not going to accept
a son-in-law who is beneath her."

"Better offer her in marriage to the sun," answered her
husband impatiently. "As far as I know, there is nothing
greater than he."

"Well, I was thinking of it," replied the wife, "and as you
are of the same mind, we will pay him a visit tomorrow."

So the next morning, the two rats, having spent hours in
making themselves smart, set out to see the sun, leading
their daughter between them.

The journey took some time, but at length they came to
the golden palace where the sun lived.

"Noble King," began the mother, "behold our daughter!
She is so beautiful that she is above everything in the whole
world. Naturally, we wish for a son-in-law who, on his side,
is greater than all. Therefore, we have come to you."

"I feel very much flattered," replied the sun, who was so
busy that he had not the least wish to marry anybody. "You
do me great honor by your proposal. Only, in one point you
are mistaken, and it would be wrong of me to take advantage of your ignorance. There is something greater than I
am, and that is the cloud. Look!" And as he spoke a cloud
spread itself over the sun's face, blotting out his rays.

"Oh, well, we will speak to the cloud," said the mother.
And turning to the cloud she repeated her proposal.

"Indeed I am unworthy of any thing so charming," answered the cloud; "but you make a mistake again in what you say. There is one thing that is even more powerful than I, and that is the wind. Ah, here he comes, you can see for yourself."

And she did see for, catching up the cloud as he passed, the wind threw it on the other side of the sky. Then, tumbling father, mother, and daughter down to earth again, he paused for a moment beside them, his foot on an old wall.

When she had recovered her breath, the mother began her little speech once more.

"The wall is the proper husband for your daughter," answered the wind, whose home consisted of a cave, which he visited only when he was not rushing about elsewhere. "You can see for yourself that he is greater than I, for he has power to stop me in my flight." And the mother, who did not trouble to conceal her wishes, turned at once to the wall.

Then, something happened that was quite unexpected by everyone.

"I won't marry that ugly old wall, which is as old as my grandfather," sobbed the girl, who had not uttered one word all this time. "I would have married the sun, or the cloud, or the wind, because it was my duty, although I love the handsome young rat, and him only. But that horrid old wall—I would sooner die!"

And the wall, his feelings rather hurt, declared that he had no claim to be the husband of so beautiful a girl.

"It is quite true," he said, "that I can stop the wind who can part the clouds who can cover the sun; but there is someone who can do more than all these, and that is the rat who lives under me. He is stronger than I am, for he can reduce me to powder, simply by gnawing with his teeth. If, therefore, you want a son-in-law who is greater than the whole world, seek him among the rats."

"Ah, what did I tell you?" cried the father. And his wife, though for the moment angry at being beaten, soon thought that a rat son-in-law was what she had always desired.

*So all three returned happily home, and the wedding
was celebrated three days after.*

USING THE FAIRY TALE IN THERAPY

This story, *The Husband of the Rat's Daughter*, is
reproduced from the *Brown Fairy Book* (Lang, 1966). Like
so much time-honored literature, it is rich in meaning. Or
perhaps it would be more accurate to say that it is rich in
possible meanings, for different people will certainly take
different meanings from it—such as beauty is in the eye of
the beholder.

I do not suggest that you should necessarily ever use this
fairy tale in precisely the form set out above. I never have.
Indeed, there is no reason why you should ever use it in
any form. There are countless other possible metaphors,
including a vast number of fairy tales. Nevertheless, I do
suggest that the accumulated wisdom stored in fairy tales
such as this is a valuable resource for therapists—and for
anyone else who wishes to put points over effectively. If
you are at a loss for an original story or other metaphor of
your own, a quick mental review of fairy tales with which
you are familiar, or a look through one or more of the many
available books of fairy tales, may provide you with the
inspiration you need. The tale you choose to use may
require some modification to suit the clinical situation in
which you plan to use it.

Let us examine the above tale to see how it might serve
as a therapeutic metaphor. Mills and Crowley (1986)
suggest that effective therapeutic metaphors have certain
ingredients:

1. A theme of "metaphorical conflict" is first established.
2. Unconscious conflicts are represented in the metaphor.
3. Parallel learning experiences are personified.
4. A metaphorical crisis is presented, leading to the

overcoming or resolution of the problem that the metaphor addresses.
5. A new sense of identification is presented.
6. The metaphor ends with a celebration.

Mills and Crowley (1986) proceed to discuss how the story of *The Ugly Duckling* meets these criteria. Let us, however, look at how the tale of *The Husband of the Rat's Daughter* does so.

1. *The metaphorical conflict.* Mr. and Mrs. Rat have a very special only child—a daughter who is so beautiful and special that, in her mother's eyes, she can be allowed only to marry someone quite exceptional. This means that her husband can be no mere rat. (One might postulate, incidentally, that Mrs. Rat was not too happy with her identity as a rat.)

2. *The unconscious processes and potentials.* Mr. Rat disagrees, believing that the daughter should marry another rat. There are pros and cons of each course of action, represented here, perhaps, by the differing views of the two parents. Both parents may be presumed to believe that what they want is also what is best for their daughter, despite the possibility that their own pride could be a factor in determining what each wishes. (How frequent it is that we therapists meet parents who cannot agree about their children!)

3. *The parallel learning situations.* Cynically, Mr. Rat suggests that their daughter should marry the sun because "there is nothing greater than he." Mrs. Rat takes him up on this and they explore the possibility. They discover that things are not quite as simple as they thought. Precisely who is the greatest is not as clear as they initially assumed. Soon they start to be presented with new information about just who may be greatest among possible husbands.

4. *The metaphorical crisis.* Neither the sun, the cloud, the wind, nor the wall is willing to marry the beautiful young girl rat. Even more unexpected, the girl rebels, saying she would rather die than marry the "ugly old wall." The parents begin to realize that however much they

believe they know what is best for their daughter, other points of view are possible and may even have merit.

5. *The new identification.* Being a rat isn't so bad after all; indeed, marrying the handsome young rat with whom the daughter was in love turns out to be the best solution after all.

6. *The celebration.* This, of course, is the wedding.

This story contains many potential meanings. It covers the all-too-common parental disagreements we so frequently encounter; the idealization of children, which sometimes leads parents to sacrifice their children's best interests to their own needs for glorification; the failure of some parents to consider their children's wishes and points of view when it might be appropriate to do so; that things are not always as simple as they sometimes seem (the sun proved not to be as great as they thought); and the point that a bit of practical investigation (the journey the family took) can yield valuable new information. And, like all good therapeutic maneuvers, this one resulted in a reframing of the problem situation—or the "new identification" of Mills and Crowley (1986). Marrying the handsome young rat "with moustaches that almost swept the ground" was not such a bad idea after all. The daughter, indeed, had been wiser from the start; only the parents' pride had stood in the way of their taking a rational position in this matter.

It is not difficult to see in the story above the possible "shared phenomenological reality" of Rossi (1985, p. 48), discussed in Chapter 5. The parental conflict, the overweening desire to control and make decisions for one's children, the pride in one's children; and the failure to consider one's children's points of view—all are contained in it. Yet they are not explicitly stated. Listeners can pick up on those points that are meaningful to them, and just enjoy the rest of the story as a rather quaint, old-fashioned fairy tale.

The Husband of the Rat's Daughter is a ready-made story that offers us something we may choose to use as a therapeutic metaphor. Indeed, it presumably was devised to convey a series of messages such as those outlined above. In clinical practice, though, it is necessary to devise or modify metaphors to suit the particular needs of each client, family, or group. However, some metaphors seem to have what one might consider almost universal applicability. *The Ugly Duckling* shows how, despairing and isolated, we later can go through a period of transition and discover that we are more than—and different from—what we thought.

The story of *Cinderella* is another tale that has the potential to be widely used as a therapeutic metaphor. Who has not at times felt a bit like Cinderella? Certainly—and sadly—many children are treated rather as Cinderella was, and not only by wicked stepmothers, though the tale does highlight a danger into which stepparents may fall. But although Cinderella was regarded as a person of little or no worth, and was treated accordingly by her stepmother, the prince saw her in quite a different light and chose her for his bride.

ISOMORPHIC SITUATIONS AND CHARACTERS

Gordon (1978) emphasizes the importance of taking note of the representational systems used by those for whom you are devising metaphors. He also stresses the importance of making metaphors isomorphic—that is similar or equivalent to the "real-life" situation that they represent. Thus, *The Husband of the Rat's Daughter* would not meet the criterion of isomorphism if the family were one in which the child was regarded in a negative light. *Cinderella* might be more appropriate. It would probably be unsuitable for use with a single parent family, though it could certainly be modified for such a family.

In a previous volume (Barker, 1985), I consider a hypothetical family, the Jones family, composed of a father, a mother, a son, a daughter, and an adopted daughter. The parents sought help because of the children's violent fights. A metaphorical scenario was then constructed, as outlined in Tables 7.1 and 7.2 reproduced from the earlier book.

TABLE 7.1
A Real-Life Family and Their Metaphoric Counterparts

Real Life	Metaphor
Father (Harold)	Father (Ivan) in newly opened foster home
Mother (Jane)	Mother (Karen)
Son (Lance), age 12	Daughter (Mary, age 16)
Daughter (Nancy), age 12	Son (Oscar), age 13
Adopted Daughter (Pamela), age 6	Foster-son (Quentin), age 5

Reprinted from Barker, P. (1985). *Using Metaphors in Psychotherapy*. New York: Brunner/Mazel. p. 47.

The next step, once the characters in the story have been created, is to develop a scenario that is isomorphic with the real-life situation. In the case of the family above, this was as follows:

TABLE 7.2
A Metaphoric Scenario

Real Life	Metaphor
Mother favors her son, Lance	Ivan always takes his daughter, Mary's, side in disputes
Lance orders his sisters about a lot	Mary is put in charge of the younger children
Nancy resents Pamela and fights with her	Oscar loses his temper with Quentin
Harold and Jane disagree over what to do about the children's fights	Ivan and Karen are at loggerheads about how to deal with the situation

Reprinted from Barker, P. (1985). *Using Metaphors in Psychotherapy*. New York: Brunner/Mazel. p. 47.

Having devised the metaphorical scenario, the next task the therapist must accomplish is that of using it to meet the therapeutic objectives for which the metaphor has been developed. This involves what Gordon (1978) calls the "connecting strategy."

How might we approach the issue that Harold and Jane disagree about what to do about the fights between Nancy and Pamela? (Let us assume that simply suggesting to Nancy and Pamela that they agree on a common plan of action has either failed or is considered unlikely to be effective, perhaps because other direct injunctions have proved ineffective.)

At times, the disagreements between Harold and Jane became quite heated. This situation might be reframed as indicating that both parents cared deeply about their children. Each was committed to being the best possible parent and each felt strongly about what was the best way of dealing with the children's fights. Unfortunately, they had lost sight of the importance and advantages of acting in concert and presenting a united front to their children. And this despite their felt commitment to being the best parents they could be! This point, presented in metaphorical form, becomes the connecting strategy.

In the metaphorical scenario to be presented to the family, Ivan and Karen were both committed to being the best possible foster parents. Yet they found themselves at loggerheads. This was explained as being a function of the deeply felt desire each had to give their very best in caring for their children, including the foster child.

Another behavior the therapy needed to address was Lance's practice of ordering his sisters around. How can that be represented and dealt with constructively in the metaphor? As with the disagreements between the parents, it is necessary to consider first what the points are that you wish to communicate through your metaphor. In the case of this family, it seemed that it would be helpful to reframe Lance's overly bossy behavior towards his sisters as evidence of his interest in them, though perhaps his

enthusiasm had got the better of him and he was overdoing
it a bit.

How might this point be incorporated in the story to be
offered to the family? The behavior of Mary (who in the
metaphorical scenario represents Lance) towards the
younger children was reframed in the metaphor. The story
was presented as an account of how a therapist had dealt
with the foster family that had been created as the metaphorical scenario. The therapist was "quoted" as saying
that he was impressed by the care Mary had been showing
to both the younger children, and by how hard she had
been trying to help them settle their differences.

A central problem in the family in this case was formulated as being that the parents were in disagreement about
how to handle their children's behavior problems. Here is
the conclusion of the metaphor (Barker, 1985):

> The parents asked the therapist which of their
> methods of dealing with the children was best or
> were both of them on the wrong track? He suggested
> they try an experiment. For one week they should
> use Ivan's methods and for the next they should use
> Karen's. They spun a coin to see whose methods
> would be used first; Karen won. The therapist's
> only stipulation was that for each week both par-
> ents would use identical methods, even if each
> disagreed with what the other one advocated. He
> made one other suggestion: they should both ob-
> serve Oscar carefully to see if they thought he was
> jealous of his foster brother. (This was because the
> question had arisen of whether Nancy, whom Oscar
> represented in the scenario, was jealous of her new
> adoptive sister.)
>
> The results of the experiment were surprising.
> The children were better behaved during both weeks,
> and the parents found it difficult to decide which
> was the better of the two weeks. This was remark-
> able because Ivan's and Karen's methods were quite
> different, Ivan's being a lot stricter. Precisely how

the children were handled didn't seem to matter as much as having Ivan and Karen work together. Despite observing Oscar closely, as their therapist had asked them to do, Ivan and Karen didn't detect much evidence of jealousy on his part; in fact, he seemed to thrive on being observed. (pp. 52–53)

In this case the "metaphorical disguise" was fairly thin. The metaphorical scenario was another family, and one in which there was a newly arrived child, as there was in the family being treated. The family might well have become consciously aware that the therapist was talking about their situation. This raises the question of how far metaphors should be recognizable as directly representing the situation of the clients to which they are presented. Like so many other questions that arise concerning psychotherapy, this is a question that cannot be answered on the basis of hard research data. Psychotherapy is as much an art as it is a science, and much depends on the degree of rapport that exists between therapist and client and on the personalities and motivation of all concerned.

When the above case is considered, there would seem to be reason to believe that a "heavy" disguise might not be required. The parents in this case were well motivated people who were keen to have help and could be expected to be open to input. What they needed was a different way of looking at their problem. Simply telling them that they should work together cooperatively had not proved sufficient. The point needed emphasizing and objectifying. By listening to a tale of how others had found a solution of a type that might be of help to them, they were able to look at their problem "from the outside." Several features of the story probably assisted them in grasping it and applying its message:

- The parents asked the therapist to help them decide which of them was on the right track, but the therapist did not take sides, instead suggesting that an experiment might help decide.

- Rather than coming down on either parent's side, the "therapist" in the metaphor took a neutral stance.

- The results were "surprising." The result was not what either parent was expecting. It reframed the issue; instead of being a matter of which parent's methods were "right" or at least better, it became a matter of whether they worked together. This is equivalent to the "new identification" stage in Mills and Crowley's (1986) analysis. The new identification thus need not be a new view that a person acquires of himself or herself; it may equally be a new understanding of a situation.

- Careful observation of "Oscar" did not reveal much evidence of jealousy on his part, but "he seemed to thrive on being observed." This might be used by the parents as a hint or suggestion that a little more attention to Nancy—whom Oscar represented—might yield dividends.

A strength of metaphorical communication is that those to whom metaphors are offered are free to take what they may and leave the rest. If, for example, the parents did not pick up on the point about Oscar thriving when he was given extra attention, nothing would have been lost.

LONG STORY, SHORT STORY, OR ANECDOTE?

Dividing long stories from short ones and short stories from anecdotes is somewhat arbitrary. The real distinction lies in whether the metaphor aims to deal comprehensively with a complex situation or simply to make a limited point or points.

The metaphor discussed above could be presented as a long story; indeed, the conclusion reprinted above consists of just the last two paragraphs of a 16-paragraph story.

Milton Erickson was a master at devising and delivering short stories to make points. He seems quite often to have told his patients about other patients he had treated who had similar symptoms. In the course of the "teaching seminar" (Zeig, 1980, pp. 58–61), Erickson spoke first of how he had helped a lawyer who wanted to move from Wisconsin to Arizona. This man had failed the Arizona bar examinations five times, despite being a well-informed lawyer who had a good practice in Wisconsin. He explained how he had used certain hypnotic techniques to enable the lawyer to pass the examinations on his sixth attempt. He went on to explain that, "...all I did was to make him think that Arizona was a nice place to live, and that the law examination was awfully unimportant; so he had no anxiety, no fear" (p. 63). He continued as follows:

> A woman had flunked her Ph.D. examination over and over again. Her committee knew that she could pass, and yet she always went into a panic and blanked out everything. So I had her sit in with a class where I told her about the lawyer and she went into a trance listening to the case about the lawyer. After I finished the report, she awakened. I dismissed her, and she went back to her home state. A month later she wrote to me: "I passed my Ph.D. exam with flying colors. What did you do to me?" (pp. 63–64)

Laughing, Erickson commented, "I didn't do anything except tell her about that lawyer."

The situation of the lawyer was, of course, a metaphor for that of the Ph.D. candidate who presumably took from it a message that enabled her to approach the examination in as anxiety- and fear-free state as the lawyer had approached his. No doubt, many people had previously told her that she knew more than enough to pass the examination. They had probably told her there was no cause for anxiety or fear. But such "advice" offered and received at the conscious level may not be effective. Metaphor, which may often usefully be combined with hypnosis (as we shall see in the next chapter), may allow the message to bypass the conscious mind and deal with the unconscious processes that are responsible for the presenting problems.

RELATIONSHIP METAPHORS

As mentioned earlier, Milton Erickson is quoted as having said, "If you want a man to tell you about his brother, tell him about yours." That, in capsule form, illustrates the principle behind the relationship metaphor.

Many who come to therapists for help have problems with relationships. There are many possible ways of approaching the treatment of such clients. Presenting the "relationship dilemma," and possible solutions to that dilemma, metaphorically is one. A quick look at stories, long and short, novels, fairy tales, and myths reveals that many, perhaps most, do address questions of relationships between people or groups of people. *The Husband of the Rat's Daughter*, for example, deals with relationships between parents—who may have trouble agreeing what is best for their children—and also with relationships between parents on the one hand and their children on the other. Yet this is not quite what I mean by "relationship metaphor."

There are many ways in which one relationship can be used as a metaphor for another. We often find, when we explore the extended family networks of our clients, relationships that may serve as metaphors for those in which our clients are involved. For example, it is not uncommon to encounter parents who, quite unconsciously, are reliving dysfunctional family scenarios similar to those in which they grew up. Another situation we may come across is that in which a couple whose marital relationship is in difficulty are, in some respects, playing out aspects of conflicts the parents of one or the other, or of both of them, struggled with when they were children.

In such cases, a careful, objective and non-blaming discussion of how their parents' marriage or their child-rearing practices got into difficulties can be helpful. It may suggest, at one remove (that is, metaphorically), some of the problem behaviors, beliefs, or attitudes responsible for our clients' current difficulties. It is often possible to go further and discuss what solutions, or alternative courses of action, or attitudes, might have been of use to their parents or to other extended family members who may be mentioned during the discussion.

Other points that might be raised include the question of what was stopping the parents or other family members from making the changes they might have made; how easy it might have been to make them; how the changes might have been accomplished; and what the likely effects of making those changes would have been.

Thus, past relationships can sometimes be used as metaphors for the dilemmas our clients currently face. Within those metaphors, new insights, and even possible solutions to their problems, may be found. Approaching these situations in this indirect, metaphorical way is usually less threatening and stimulates less resistance than a direct discussion of how our clients may have made poor choices and overlooked possibly better courses of action.

Here is another way of using a relationship as a metaphor:

> I remember so well, even though it is many years ago, an episode while I was a medical student in a teaching hospital in London, England. Generally, I was a good student, favorably regarded by my teachers. I usually received good reports at the end of the various periods of practical experience we had to undergo in the course of our three years of clinical experience and training. The big exception—one that stands out in my mind—was my six weeks in the emergency department.
>
> I did not get along at all well with the nurse in charge in the emergency department. I felt justified

in this because this nurse had a reputation for being a difficult person to get along with and for having a low regard for medical students. She seemed to feel they were a burden and that the department would have run better without them (as indeed it might have). This nurse and I clashed repeatedly, and I must confess that on a number of occasions I was less than courteous to her.

The result—predictable, I suppose, though I had not expected it—was that I received, at the end of the six weeks, an unfavorable report on my time in the department. As a consequence, and much to my chagrin, I found myself summoned to the office of the dean of the medical school to explain my poor showing in the emergency department. I did my best to account for the problems and to justify myself on the basis of the "atmosphere" for students in the department, without overtly criticizing the nurse in charge. It seemed clear to me, though, that the dean knew perfectly well what I was referring to. He then asked me: "Do you think the trouble was related to a clash of personalities?"

Relieved that it seemed as if it was that clash, not me, that would be held responsible for the problems, I replied in the affirmative.

It didn't get me off the hook, though.

"I hope you can learn an important lesson from this, Barker," he said. "You'll find that this clash of personalities will prove to be only one of many difficult relationships you will encounter over the years. There will be people whom you will find it hard to get on with in all sorts of situations—in your work and outside it. And there will be people who find you hard to get along with, too.

"It's our job to deal constructively with the situations in which we find ourselves. Difficult people—and there are plenty of them—are challenges to our maturity and social skills. There is no excuse for engaging them in battle, and if you do, everyone loses. Next time this happens, I hope that instead of getting caught up in destructive conflict, you will give some thought to how you can handle the situation constructively, not destructively."

I'm sure I haven't quoted the dean's exact words, but his message has remained with me ever since. His advice has proved to be some of the best I have ever received.

This is a true story that I have found can be useful with older children and adolescents who complain about their teachers; or with employees who have trouble getting on with their bosses; or with just about anyone who gets into a conflictual relationship and is feeling justified in engaging in the conflict. It can be embellished, if need be, by my describing how outraged I felt at the time that the dean did not take my side against the nurse about whom I was, as I felt, quite justifiably complaining. In reality, it was only later, after I had had time to reflect, that I realized that there might be something of value in what the dean told me. Indeed, it was only over a period of years that the full value of his advice became clear to me. The latter is a point I emphasize if I feel that the person to whom I am telling the story will take a while to integrate and make full use of the metaphor.

Married couples may be stuck in mutually blaming ways of relating, with much recrimination and criticism. The conflicts may be over how their children should be raised, how they should manage their financial affairs, or even simply about where they should go on vacation. Each partner believes that he or she has the better idea or plan of action; neither will consider the other's point of view as having merit.

How might we set about devising a therapy plan using metaphor for such situations? The world is full of examples of warring parties who have come to see the futility of continued conflict. Examples that might be used as metaphors during treatment range from the end of apartheid in South Africa to the reconciliation of local figures likely to be known to your clients. In Canada we had a running battle for many months between our two major airlines, Air Canada and Canadian Airlines International. Fare wars, verbal slanging matches, appeals to government regulators and agencies, and lawsuits, launched and threatened, characterized relationships between the two airlines for month after month. The energies of the boards and top officials of each of the airlines seemed to be devoted mainly to the battle, seemingly at the expense of working to make their respective airlines profitable. Eventually, early in 1994—presumably because each had at last realized the destructiveness of their conflict—common sense prevailed, and the airlines buried the hatchet and seemed willing to get on with the job of providing services for travelers.

TASKS, RITUALS, AND METAPHORICAL OBJECTS

The definitive work on therapeutic rituals is *Rituals in Families and Family Therapy* (Imber-Black et al., 1988), although the value of rituals is not confined to family therapy. Imber-Black et al. distinguish "five ritual themes"—that is to say, five types of clinical situations in which rituals may be of value. These are:

- Membership themes
- Healing themes
- Identity definition and redefinition
- Belief expression and negotiation
- Celebration

It would not be correct to regard all the rituals that may be used in therapy as necessarily being metaphors. But many are. Let us consider membership rituals. These include not only such events as weddings, baptisms, bar mitzvahs, and graduation ceremonies, but also family

meals eaten together and recreational activities undertaken as a family or as a group. A baptism is clearly a
ceremony at which the baptized person is welcomed into
the religious group concerned in a way that is direct rather
than metaphorical—though it has metaphorical elements
such as the sprinkling on, or immersion in, water. On the
other hand, the family meal taken together—or not, as the
case may be—can be a powerful metaphor for the way a
family functions. Imber-Black et al. (1988) offers us the
following example:

> In one divorced family, the three sons complained
> that the family had not had a meal together "since
> Father left." Instead, the mother cooked and ate in
> her room alone, while the oldest and youngest son
> ate in front of the television at separate times and
> the middle son stayed out on the streets during
> dinner. This daily ritual replaced the one of the
> family eating together and served as a painful meta-
> phor for the family's current fragmentation. (p. 51)

The above quotation suggests how meal times might be
used metaphorically. The possibility exists of explaining
to a family such as the above that they have become
fragmented. The advantages of becoming a more unified
group of mutually supportive people could be pointed out,
and they could be advised to do things together and talk
among themselves more. For some families, this might
prove helpful but we have seen that direct injunctions may
fail to produce change; in that case suggesting that the
family have a meal, or meals, together may be a metaphorical way of tackling the problem.

Fragmentation can lead to unfortunate results. An example of this is contained in the biography of the great New
Orleans clarinetist, George Lewis (Bethel, 1977). Lewis
was a member of Bunk Johnson's band, which in 1945
came from New Orleans to play at the Stuyvesant Casino
in New York. The band consisted of old-time musicians
who had been living in obscurity in Louisiana, for the most

part since the onset of the great depression, until they were "rediscovered" and recorded by a few dedicated jazz enthusiasts. This led to their being engaged to come to New York, with the prospect of much wider recognition than any of them had ever received before. This great opportunity was partially wasted because they never seemed to have become a happy family. Here is a brief excerpt from Bethel (1977):

> The band hired a woman named Clementine from New Orleans . . . to cook for them . . . Characteristically, Bunk did not go along with this. He would shop for himself and come back from his solitary expeditions with culinary odds and ends that he carefully labeled and kept in a separate corner of the icebox. (p. 200)

It is small wonder that there were serious tensions on the bandstand, turning a great opportunity into something of a disaster. This is another example, which may be used as a metaphor, of the unfortunate situation that arises when people do not eat (or work, or live, or play) together.

Imber-Black et al. (1988) present a wealth of examples of how rituals may be used. They often involve the use of metaphorical objects. These may be buried, burned, preserved frozen, or—in hypnotic trance—allowed to float up into the sky attached to a helium balloon until they become but a tiny speck in the distance and, finally, cannot be seen at all. The book not only offers rituals for the five categories of clinical situations mentioned above, but also discusses how rituals may be used with couples, children, adolescents, issues of multigenerational change and continuity, families with adopted members, and alcoholic families; it also discusses their use in sex therapy, in the creation of family identity, and in wider social contexts.

As with the other forms of metaphor, there is nothing new about the setting of tasks. The Buddha was quite familiar with these, as the following tale told of him illustrates:

A woman named Kisa Gotami had a young son who was the sunshine of her day. But hardly had he grown big enough to run when illness struck him and he died. So great was Kisa Gotami's sorrow that she could not accept her boy's death. Instead she took to the streets, carrying her dead son on her hip. She went from house to house, knocking on each door and demanding: "Give me medicine for my son."

People, seeing her as mad, made fun of her and told her that there was no medicine for the dead. But she did not seem to understand and continued to ask.

Then, a wise old man saw Kisa Gotami and understood that it was her sorrow that had driven her out of her mind. Instead of mocking her he told her: "Woman, the only one who might know of medicine for your son is the Possessor of Ten Forces, he who is foremost among men and gods. Go then to the monastery. Go then to him and ask about medicine for your son."

Seeing that the wise man spoke the truth, she went with her son on her hip to the monastery in which the Buddha resided. Eagerly she approached the Seat of the Buddhas where the teacher sat. "I wish to have medicine for my son, Exalted One," she said.

Smiling serenely, the Buddha answered: "It is well that you have come here. This is what you must do. You must go to each house in the city, one by one, and from each you must seek to fetch tiny grains of mustard seeds. But not just any house will do. You must take mustard seeds only from those houses in which no one had ever died."

Gotami at once set out and reentered the city. At the first house she knocked and asked, saying: "It is I, Gotami, sent by the Possessor of the Ten Forces. You are to give me a tiny mustard seed. This is the medicine I must have for my son." And when they

brought her the mustard seed, she added: "Before I
take the seed, tell me, is this a house in which no one
has died?" "Oh no, Gotami," they answered, "the
dead in this house are beyond counting." "Then I
must go elsewhere," said Gotami. "The Exalted One
was very clear that I must seek out seeds only from
houses in which no one has died."

Gotami continued her search but in the whole
city she found not one house in which no one had
died. Finally she understood why she had been sent
on this hopeless mission. She left the city, overcome with feeling, and carried her dead son to the
burial ground, where she gave him up.

Returning to the monastery, she was greeted by
the softly smiling Buddha, who asked her: "Good
Gotami, did you fetch the tiny grains of mustard
seed from the houses without death, as I told you?"

Gotami answered: "Most honored sir, there are
no houses where death is not known. All mankind
is touched by death. But now I see that whoever is
born must die. Everything passes away. There is no
medicine for this but acceptance of it. There is no
cure but the knowing. My search for the mustard
seeds is over. You, O Possessor of the Ten Forces,
have given me refuge. Thank you, my Exalted One."

In a sense, the mustard seeds that did not exist (those
from houses in which no one had died) were metaphorical
objects, in that they carried a message by their nonexis-
tence. Another use of metaphorical objects is as part of
"termination rituals"—that is, rituals used at the termination of therapy and that represent symbolically the therapy
process that has taken place.

EXTERNALIZING THE PROBLEM

This device, while perhaps not strictly metaphorical, is
closely related. It was developed by Michael White and is
described in White and Epston (1990). White describes

externalizing as "an approach to therapy that encourages persons to objectify and, at times, to personify the problems they experience as oppressive."

Symptoms are explored for what may be behind them, for example "guilt" or "insecurity." An as an illustration of this method, White and Epston (1990) take a case of encopresis. The patient was a six-year-old boy who had a long history of soiling that had defeated all attempts at treatment. The boy had "befriended" the "poo" and was playing with it, streaking it down walls, rolling it into balls, plastering it under the kitchen table. The poo was making the boy's and his mother's life a misery, embarrassing his father, and affecting all relationships within the family. When its widespread effects became recognized, it was considered to merit the title of "Sneaky Poo."

After Sneaky Poo's adverse influences on the family had been carefully explored and agreement on this had been reached among the family members, the therapist encouraged the family members to consider how they might "outsmart" or even defeat Sneaky Poo. The boy decided he would no longer be tricked into being Sneaky Poo's playmate. His mother thought up some new ideas that would help her refuse to let Sneaky Poo push her into a state of misery, and his father decided he might just manage to tell a coworker about his struggle with Sneaky Poo. The family was successful in outsmarting and outrunning Sneaky Poo, and the boy's symptoms were alleviated. For a full account of this case, and the method of which it is an example, see Chapter 2 in White and Epston (1990).

The above has become something of a celebrated case, but the concepts on which it is based can be applied to a wide variety of problems and several other examples are to be found in Chapter 2 of White and Epston (1990) as well.

ARTISTIC METAPHORS

Mills and Crowley (1986), in *Therapeutic Metaphors for Children and the Child Within,* offer us a variety of ideas about how we may use artistic productions and activities in therapy. Most children enjoy drawing and painting, as well as using modelling materials. Many children present us, in their artistic productions, with metaphors about their feelings, views of life, and understanding of situations they or others face. The very size and scale of their drawings can tell us much about them. The fearful, inhibited child may draw a tiny picture in one corner of a piece of paper; the angry, acting-out child may fill the entire sheet with symbols of aggression. Much has been written about the interpretation of children's drawings, for example by DiLeo (1983).

Mills and Crowley (1986) have carried the use of drawings and other artistic productions further. They invite children to express their feelings by drawing them. Children can be asked to draw "afraid" and "all better." By asking the child what "all better" will look like, the therapist implies—in metaphor—that the symptoms can get better, and in drawing "all better" the child signifies unconscious agreement that "I can make it better."

This method can be applied to virtually any feeling state or situation children—or theoretically even adults—may face, for example, anger, loneliness, despair, sadness or depression, and pain. For pain control, Mills and Crowley (1986, pp. 174–179) describe their use of the "pain getting better book." This book involves three steps:

1. How the pain looks right now.
2. How the pain will look "all better."
3. What will help Picture One change into Picture Two.

This process is designed, first, to help the child dissociate from the pain. By drawing it, the child may be enabled, at least to some extent, to dissociate from it. It is now on the piece of paper on which it has been drawn, rather than in the child. Some distance from the pain is thus created.

Mills and Crowley's second point is that "giving the pain a tangible image gives the child a sense of knowing what she is dealing with—of moving from the unknown to the known" (p. 179).

The third point these authors make is that giving pain a visual representation switches attention from one sensory channel to another—from the kinesthetic to the visual. "Drawing what the pain looks like helps activate other parts of the brain which diffuse attention and provide a wealth of helpful resources" (p. 179).

Finally, the drawings use the power of implication. The very act of drawing the pain (or for that matter any other unwelcome feeling) "all better" implies that the state of "all better" can and does exist.

Cartoon therapy, described in Chapter 8 of Mills and Crowley (1986) has aims rather similar to those of artistic metaphors. Many children look at cartoons in newspapers and other publications, and even more watch them on television. I have been impressed, also, by the number of children who like to draw cartoons and even have the ambition to be cartoonists when they grow up. When one is working with such children, the cartoon can be a powerful therapeutic tool. Children engaged in conflictual relationship with others may be asked to illustrate these in cartoon drawings. They can then be asked to draw a series of cartoon episodes showing the characters resolving their differences and to end with a picture of the reconciled subjects doing something pleasurable together. None of this need be explicitly related to the real-life situation of the child being treated, but the metaphorical meaning may have powerful significance. And again, as with metaphors generally, nothing is lost if the child does not pick up on the potential meaning of the metaphor.

Mills and Crowley (1986) provide many illustrations both of the use of artistic metaphors and of cartoon therapy, and the book is recommended to the reader wishing to explore these approaches further.

SUMMARY

Fairy tales are a rich source of metaphorical material. Typically they present conflicts in metaphorical terms and proceed to show how the conflicts may be resolved. If we take care to ensure that the situations and characters in fairy tales we use are, to a reasonable degree, isomorphic with the real-life situations of our clients, they can be powerful change-promoting tools. Major stories of our own creation can be used in similar fashion.

Short stories and anecdotes can be similarly effective but have more limited aims. Relationships, including those between members of clients' extended families, and between therapist and client(s), or between therapist and someone else, can be used as metaphors for other relationships. Metaphorical meaning may also be built into tasks and rituals, some of which use objects as metaphors for problem symptoms or situations, or as reminders of the process of therapy after this has been successfully completed.

"Externalizing"—and even personifying—problems, including problem relationships, and expressing and exploring them through artistic productions and/or cartoons may be of particular value in work with children.

8

TECHNICAL ASPECTS OF THE DELIVERY OF METAPHORS

When videocassette recorders were first marketed for use in the home, there were two competing systems. One was called BETA and the other VHS. At first, it was not clear which would become the standard, but it was apparent early on that there would not be room in the marketplace for two mutually incompatible systems.

Before it was clear which system would prevail in the marketplace, I sought the advice of several experts with technical knowledge in the field. Their unanimous opinion was that the BETA system was the better of the two. Despite this, it was the VHS system that gained popularity at the expense of the BETA system. VHS became the standard for home use and nowadays it is hard to find a BETA tape in most video rental stores or to buy a BETA videocassette recorder for use at home—though I understand that the BETA system is still quite widely used in industry.

It seems that the better system failed to become the standard for domestic use. How could this have come to pass? The fact seems to be that "It's not what you're selling, it's how you're selling it."

Apparently the VHS system was marketed better than the BETA system. Why that was, and how it came about,

I don't know. What it seems to show, though, is the importance of how things are presented. And when you consider the amount of advertising to which we are all subjected, and the great cost that must be involved, it is apparent that the efficient marketing of products is vital for their success. If that were not so, firms would not engage in the mass advertising that they do.

Of course, if a product is of poor quality or doesn't do the job its makers claim for it, good marketing and advertising won't compensate. The notorious car that the Ford Motor Company introduced with great fanfare—the Edsel—was fundamentally flawed. All the Ford Motor Company's marketing and advertising skills could not save what was basically a poor product. But skillful presentation of a first-rate product, well adapted to its intended purpose, is a hard combination to beat.

The message above is, of course, that to be successful in business you must both have a good product and advertise and market it well. Unless both these criteria are met, your business will probably fail.

Exactly the same applies to the construction and delivery of therapeutic metaphors. The delivery of the metaphor is as important as its content. The most brilliant metaphor, poorly delivered, may have little or no effect.

PREREQUISITES FOR SUCCESSFUL DELIVERY OF METAPHORS

What are the major prerequisites for the successful delivery of metaphors? I suggest the following:

1. There must be an adequate level of rapport between therapist and client(s).
2. The client(s) must be prepared for the use of whatever category of metaphorical message it is that you plan to use.
3. Clear therapeutic goals should have been established and agreed to with the client(s).

4. The therapist must have confidence in the therapy plan. A halfhearted or semiapologetic introduction of a metaphor (or of any other therapeutic device) is unlikely to meet with success.
5. There should be an agreed or implied contract to use indirect methods, such as metaphor, with the client(s) concerned.
6. Any appropriate steps should have been taken to ensure that the client(s) are in as receptive a state as possible.
7. Timing is an important consideration. You should consider carefully just when to introduce your metaphor, and how to pace its delivery.
8. The continuous assessment of the feedback your clients are offering you is essential. As your metaphor is being delivered, you should constantly assess the responses—principally the nonverbal ones—it is getting.
9. Thought should be given to whether it may be best to offer a metaphor based on fact or on fiction.
10. You should be clear whether you are aiming to make a single point or to embed multiple messages in what you deliver.

Let us now consider the above points in more detail.

1. Rapport

We have already discussed the importance of rapport and how its development may be promoted. Time and effort devoted to the promotion and consolidation of rapport are always well spent. Insufficient rapport may be the single most important cause of psychotherapeutic failure.

2. Preparation

Clients need to be prepared for stories and other metaphors. If you have not been in the habit of telling your clients stories, they may be surprised—even suspicious—

if you suddenly produce one. Stories can readily be incorporated into the early, rapport-building stages of therapy. They need have no special therapeutic aim other than to solidify the therapeutic relationship and promote rapport. They can often be introduced, quite naturally, by phrases such as, "You might be interested to hear about . . ." or "That reminds me of something I heard the other day. . . ." A story or two may be told quite casually at the beginning of the session, before the "serious business" gets going, or at the end, with a phrase such as, "We seem to have a minute or two left, so I'd like to tell you about. . . ."

If this happens during each session, your clients are not likely to be surprised by hearing yet another story. Then, when one offers a metaphorical message, it can be expected to be received without its purpose being questioned.

Much the same applies to other forms of metaphor, whether they be tasks set, rituals prescribed, or artistic activities suggested. If they are made a part of the activities of each, or at least most, therapy sessions, they will come to be accepted with little or no questioning. In some cases it is appropriate initially to prescribe activities with direct, rather than indirect or strategic, aims. This will tell you whether the clients can make use of direct input. When, subsequently, tasks or activities with metaphorical potential are prescribed, they will usually be accepted without much, or any, question.

Sometimes, a metaphorical task or ritual can follow another sort of intervention, for example, a paradoxical directive.

> The parents of two brothers—we'll call them Adam and Bruce—complained that the boys were constantly "fighting," which meant that they were continually arguing, shouting at each other and complaining at, and about, each other. Their parents had tried everything and indeed had attended parenting courses and received much counseling from a variety of professionals. No matter what the

parents did in their attempts to resolve the boys' disagreements, they had no success whatsoever. No matter how hard they tried, they had been unable, as they put it, to get their sons "to bury the hatchet."

More of the same therapy did not seem to be indicated. The therapist then suggested that, as the boys clearly had a need to argue and were in disagreement on a number of things, a time should be set aside each evening for them to argue, shout— at each other—even swear, if they felt like it. A minimum of five minutes was prescribed and the boys were implored to try and keep the arguing going for at least this length of time; they could continue longer if they needed to, though the therapist expressed the opinion that longer than 15 minutes probably wouldn't be required. Adam immediately objected, saying that he was sure he could carry on stating his complaints about Bruce for a much longer time. Bruce, of course, also disagreed and a fight started to get under way. The therapist cut the boys short, pointing out that this would be a suitable topic for their first "prescribed" period together. He also suggested that the parents should in future, instead of telling the boys to stop arguing and shouting at each other, simply tell them to delay this until the appointed time.

As often happens when the symptom is prescribed, the boys found it hard, after the first few evenings, to keep up their arguments, even for the five-minute minimum. The therapist increased the pressure at each meeting with the family but the boys seemed to lose interest in arguing. Eventually, the therapist observed, in an aside to the parents, that it seemed that maybe the boys were ready at last "to bury the hatchet." The boys were not familiar with this phrase, or the North American Indian ceremony to which it refers. They were therefore told about this and each agreed to construct a wooden model of a hatchet.

They then dug a hole and literally buried the hatchets in
the same "grave."

3. Establishing goals

We have seen, in Chapter 6, that it is necessary to have
clearly defined goals before embarking on treatment. The
decision to use metaphor in therapy presupposes that you
have a specific objective in mind. You should be clear
about what this is before you construct your metaphor.

One of the advantages of using metaphor is that it leaves
open the use that the person to whom it is offered makes of
it. A metaphor may not achieve the goals you have in mind,
but if it does not, you have acquired useful new information. You know more about what does not work and are
free either to devise another metaphor or to use some other
therapeutic approach. If, however, you are unsure of your
goals, you will be equally unsure of whether they were
achieved.

4. Having confidence in the therapy plan

One of the biggest difficulties some therapists seem to
have in using metaphor is in acquiring the necessary
confidence. Those of us who are used to other approaches
to therapy and have not been trained in this approach may
initially feel ill at ease in launching into a fairy tale or a
story about computers. When I meet a therapist who feels
this way, I sometimes recount my own experience of
starting to use paradoxical directives.

I tell them how initially I found it hard to pluck up the
necessary courage to suggest to my patients that they
should so something that was the very opposite of that
which I believed they really ought to do. This was despite
a conscious realization that the patients concerned were in
the habit of reacting to suggestions by doing the opposite
of what was suggested. I explain how I was reassured by the
literature on the subject, and by hearing of successful
paradoxical interventions that had been used by my super-

visor and my colleagues. Eventually, I explain, I took the plunge and was amazed at both how easy it was and how effective it sometimes proved to be. Perhaps I was lucky that the first time I used this technique it worked well, but it was clear that the anticipation was more difficult than the procedure itself.

5. The agreed or implied contract

This is related to Point 3. We will consider the ethics of the use of metaphor in Chapter 10. It is important that the therapist using any form of indirect communication or suggestion start with a clear agreement on the objectives of the therapy.

I sometimes describe therapy to my patients as a journey. Kopp (1971) makes a similar point when he likens the psychotherapist to a "guru" whom he describes as "a spiritual guide who helps others to move from one phase of their lives to another." Our lives are journeys and we do not always travel a straight road. "Sometimes," I may say to my patients, "it means taking quite a roundabout route. It may even be so twisted and turning that you wonder what direction you are headed in."

It may be helpful to talk about how those embarked on a therapy exercise—therapists as well as clients—may sometimes feel as if they are running around in a maze, and it comes as quite a relief when they finally find their way out.

The above is but a metaphor for the process of strategic therapy.

6. Promoting receptive states in clients

If you have attended properly to the points made in the previous five sections, your client will probably be in a receptive state. That is to say, if a good degree of rapport exists, if the client has become accustomed to your telling stories or prescribing rituals, if the goals of therapy have been defined and agreed on, if you are feeling confident

and if your client is aware that therapy can be a compli-
cated process that does not always lead directly from the
present state to the desired one—if all these criteria are
met, your client is probably in a receptive state.

Are there any other steps that may help? Yes, there may
be. A question to consider is whether or not to use hypnosis as an adjunct. It is widely agreed that people tend to be
more suggestible in trance than in the normal alert state.
My experience is that metaphors delivered to subjects who
are in at least a light trance state tend to have more impact.

Yet this is not as big an issue as it might seem to be. As
Lankton and Lankton (1983) point out, "Fixation of attention is itself a minimal alteration in consciousness and
produces signs of light trance" (p. 131). In other words,
once your client has started to concentrate on a story you
are telling, and attention is fixated on the story, a state of
trance already exists. While there might be some dispute as
to when concentration on something—or "fixation of attention," if you prefer—becomes hypnosis, in reality there
is no clear distinction. States of light trance, which are light
degrees of hypnosis, are commonplace. There can be few
if any people who have never experienced them.

Our question thus becomes one of whether we should
take active steps to deepen the state of trance that occurs
naturally when anyone is concentrated on listening to a
story or on carrying out a task with careful attention to
detail—or, indeed, becomes engrossed in anything. This is
a matter of clinical judgment, but I have found that hypnosis can be a valuable adjunct, especially when a planned,
carefully constructed metaphor is being offered to a client
who has been having difficulty making desired changes.

Although hypnosis can be presented in various ways,
not all of which involve the use of the term "hypnosis"—
for example, "relaxation and guided imagery"—I believe it
is better to be quite frank and explain that one plans to use
hypnosis and why. The reason I give is—quite simply—
that it is easier for many people to make changes when in
the hypnotic state than in their more usual alert state.

Many people are aware of how difficult it is to change some of their behaviors despite a strong desire to do so. Hypnosis may be presented as helping overcome this problem. Stories of people who have prevailed in various endeavors by using outflanking techniques (the German army's outflanking of the Maginot Line—(see Chapter 2)—being an example) may be helpful here. So may accounts of how hypnosis has enabled others to make desired changes that they had failed to achieve by conscious efforts in their usual "alert"—that is, nonhypnotic—state.

While some people undoubtedly have concerns about hypnosis, this is often due to a lack of information on it, or to misinformation. Some of this comes from witnessing the work of stage hypnotists, and a careful explanation of the differences between stage hypnotism and clinical hypnotherapy may clear up misunderstanding and result in the client becoming open to hypnotherapy. I find that once the issues about which clients are concerned are dealt with—and this may require more than one session—they often prove to be particularly good subjects who do well in therapy.

7. Timing

Deciding just when to offer a therapeutic metaphor is a matter of clinical judgment. No hard-and-fast rules exist. The requirements of paragraphs 1 to 6 above should, however, have been met, and your client(s) should appear to be in a receptive mood. I usually deliver metaphors soon after the need becomes apparent or a situation seems to exist in which a metaphor may be helpful—provided I have a suitable metaphor ready. But it is a mistake to go ahead before you are satisfied that your metaphor is properly designed.

Sufficient time should be left in the session for you to be able to deliver your metaphor—if it is a story or anecdote, or if it involves explaining a task or ritual in detail—in an unhurried fashion. It can also be helpful to deliver it at the end of the session. Metaphorical input seems often to have most impact when offered at the end of a session. Timing is discussed further in Chapter 9.

8. Assessing feedback

Carefully observing the feedback your clients are offering enables you to assess how your messages are being received. Most of this feedback is nonverbal. A basic issue is whether or not the client's attention is still fixed on the story or task. Also important are the nonverbal indications of changes in the client's emotional state. These may be anything from tears to expressions of joy. Movements that appear to be involuntary—often called ideomotor responses—are often observed while subjects are deeply involved in processing information. While it may not be clear exactly what is going on within the subject, the fact that attention is fixed on the metaphor being offered, and that there are ideomotor responses, can usually be taken to mean that what is being offered is being processed.

9. Fact or fiction?

Should one use a true story or a fictional one? We have considered this question in Chapter 5. It probably matters little, but the use of present or ongoing situations can be particularly powerful in therapy. So when opportunities to use current events and happenings as metaphors arise, it is best to use them. When these opportunities are taken, the metaphor can often be incorporated very naturally into the conversation, as in the following example:

> In one family I saw, the parents complained that their children were constantly fighting. Telling them not to do so, however it was done, had proved quite ineffective. At that time there had been fighting between the warring factions in the former Yugoslavia for about two years, and the United Nations had passed many resolutions calling for cease-fires, none of which had been heeded. I remarked that the parents were a bit like the U.N.

calling for cease-fires in Bosnia. I observed that I found it remarkable that the U.N. kept on doing basically the same things—talking and passing resolutions—despite the fact that they had no effect.

This led to a discussion of what the U.N. might do, or might have done, differently in order to be more effective. I suggested that if they really wanted to stop the fighting, they should take some decisive action. The discussion of what that might be seemed to give the parents a new perspective on their family situation, and they did indeed subsequently change their approach from issuing ineffective orders to their children to one involving action, with gratifying results.

Here is another example of using a current happening:

Calgary, where I have worked for the last 15 years, is noted for, among other things, its hot air balloons. There are frequent races and in the summer, when the weather is good, few days pass without at least one or two balloons floating across the city sky. They often sail past the window of my office and sometimes they come so close that one can see the occupants at work in the baskets that hang below the balloons.

One day I was talking with an 11-year-old boy who had been experiencing difficulty in school. Although of above average intelligence, his academic performance had been patchy. He would display spurts of enthusiasm in school, but after a week or two of serious application to his studies he would slip back into a state of apathy in which he achieved little or nothing.

We were talking about Eric's school difficulties when a balloon appeared outside the window. It was quite close and we could see its two occupants as the balloon glided smoothly and gracefully past. Also visible were the periodic bursts of flame as the men navigating the balloon adjusted the burner to ensure that it provided the exact amount of heat to keep the balloon at the required height.

Eric observed that the balloon was flying at a constant height. "I wonder how they keep it going so smoothly like that," he commented.

"I think that they are constantly watching to see whether it is beginning to sink lower and as soon as it does they turn up the heat to keep it up. It looks to me as if they have had a lot of experience and know just how much heat to give it at each particular moment. It's a good thing they do; otherwise, the balloon might go crashing to the ground and they might get hurt."

As we spoke, several more balloons came into view. It looked as if they were taking part in a race. I observed that some seemed to be more successful in keeping at a steady height and this led to a discussion of hot air ballooning and what it takes to win a race. This was not a subject of which I had much knowledge, but I did offer Eric my understanding of what hot air ballooning involves, namely observing wind currents and being aware of signs that indicate the location of those that are most favorable. I said that I thought it was essential for the balloonists to be constantly vigilant and to be ready at all times to adjust their height to the prevailing conditions. If they did not, they would be overtaken by others who were doing this. They might even fall to the ground and be eliminated from the race early.

As we talked, Eric became quite engrossed in his study of the balloons passing by. He seemed to be observing carefully the activities of the balloonists and commented on their respective skills—at least as he understood them. By the end of the session we had discussed at length the importance, in ballooning, of keeping one's attention on one's task. No let up is possible if the balloon's smooth progress is to be maintained and it is to have a good chance of winning the race.

The above is an example of serendipity. I had no idea that there was to be a balloon race. The balloons just appeared, although this is not an unusual happening in Calgary. On this occasion however, the youngster I was seeing reacted with obvious interest and this led to the conversation recounted above. As we talked, the metaphorical possibilities of the situation occurred to me. Here was a boy who, were he to attempt to fly a hot air balloon in the same way as he approached many of life's tasks, would soon crash to the ground. The therapeutic possibilities of this situation were evident and I decided to take advantage of them.

Was this metaphor effective? I can give no certain answer to this question. I can say, though, that Eric's school performance improved considerably during the subsequent months. Whether it would have improved anyway I have no way of knowing. Eric had been in therapy for about two months before the "balloon incident" and continued to see me after it. During this time, other therapeutic input was offered and it is impossible to say what helped—or even if anything did. I believe it is safe to say, however, that our discussion about hot air ballooning did no harm. Even if it had no effect as a therapeutic metaphor, it was a positive interaction with my patient which, at the very least, had some rapport-building value. In other words it was a "fail-safe" intervention. There was nothing to lose by using it.

For more literal-minded, concrete-thinking people, real-life events, even current ones, may be the more suitable vehicles for metaphorical messages, but for many others fiction, including fairy tales, may be effective. Children, especially, love fairy tales. Adults who read a lot or engage in creative activities such as drama or music often respond well to fictional material. It can also be helpful to note your clients' own metaphors and pick up on them. Find out what their interests and hobbies are, and also what their work involves, and consider using metaphors derived from their interests.

10. Offering multiple messages

Metaphors need not deliver only one message. Erickson would often start to tell a story, then break off before he had completed it, going on to something else, before returning to complete the story.

Lankton and Lankton (1983) discussed this use of what they called "multiple embedded metaphors." The procedure is represented in Figure 8.1.

This procedure is used in conjunction with hypnosis. Some training in clinical hypnosis is a prerequisite for the use of multiple embedded metaphors. Its first stage is the induction of hypnotic trance. Many methods, formal and informal, of inducing trance exist. A deep trance state is not usually required, however. Informal, conversational trance induction methods can often be employed to good effect. (See, for example, Hammond, 1992).

In the second stage of this procedure, a metaphor is offered that matches the situation of the client. In other words, this presents the dilemma over which the client is seeking help. Rather than immediately offering a solution, though, the therapist proceeds to Stage 3, which is designed to help the client mobilize the resources needed to resolve the problem presented in Stage 2. Stage 4, the delivery of the initial parts of further metaphors with the same objective as in Stage 3, may or may not be required.

Stage 5, called by the Lanktons "direct work," tackles directly what Erickson called "the core of the neurosis." As the Lanktons explain the term "direct" refers not to the nature of the interventions but to their target (pp. 151–152). The target is the problem believed to be behind the presenting symptoms. Thus, the anorexic patient's basic problem may be one of body image or self-esteem, and so the "direct work" would address those problems rather than the failure to eat.

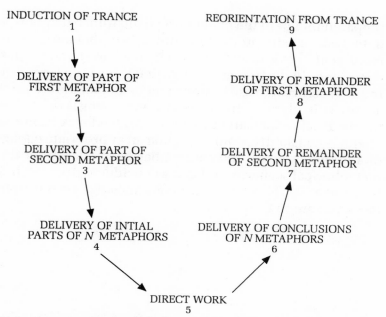

INDUCTION OF TRANCE
1

DELIVERY OF PART OF
FIRST METAPHOR
2

DELIVERY OF PART OF
SECOND METAPHOR
3

DELIVERY OF INTIAL
PARTS OF *N* METAPHORS
4

DIRECT WORK
5

DELIVERY OF CONCLUSIONS
OF *N* METAPHORS
6

DELIVERY OF REMAINDER
OF SECOND METAPHOR
7

DELIVERY OF REMAINDER
OF FIRST METAPHOR
8

REORIENTATION FROM TRANCE
9

Figure 8.1. The multiple embedded metaphor process. (Adapted with permission from Lankton & Lankton, 1983.)

In Stages 6 and 7, the metaphors begun in Stages 3 and 4 are concluded. Then, in Stage 8, the metaphor started in Stage 2 is completed, following which the client is reorientated from trance.

This is an advanced procedure that one should not attempt without some training in hypnotic techniques and before becoming familiar with and comfortable in the use of simpler metaphorical methods.

Lankton and Lankton (1983, pp. 247–311) provide a detailed account of how to use this procedure, with transcripts of clinical examples.

SUMMARY

The successful delivery of metaphors during psychotherapy requires that a good degree of rapport exist between therapist and client(s); that clients are properly prepared for use of the metaphorical medium (story, anecdote, task, artistic production and so on); that clear treatment goals have been agreed on; that the therapist has confidence in the treatment plan; that there is an agreed or implied contract to use indirect methods; that the client(s) are in a suitably receptive state; that the timing is right; that the feedback, especially the nonverbal feedback from the client, is constantly monitored; that an appropriate choice of a fictional or real-life context has been chosen for the metaphorical scenario; and that a considered decision has been taken as to whether a single message or multiple messages are to be offered.

9

PITFALLS AND HOW TO
AVOID THEM

As well as being a psychiatrist, I have a business as a record producer. In February, 1994, I travelled to Portland, Oregon, to supervise a recording session by a jazz trio.

I had some misgivings as I prepared to go to the recording studio. We had only about five hours of studio time to record the material for an entire compact disc—a very short time. I had met only one of the three musicians involved—Jessica Williams, the pianist. I had had no previous acquaintance with the others—bass player Jeff Johnson and drummer Dick Berk. I knew that the session could be—almost certainly would be—a disaster if there were not a good level of rapport between the musicians.

Jessica Williams had assured me that she had played with these musicians many times before and that they worked well together. I was glad about that but not completely reassured.

In the event, the recording session went extraordinarily well. I found that these were three musicians in perfect rapport. In the allotted five hours, they recorded more than enough music for the CD. Particularly impressive to me was their performance of a tune called "Nommo." It was stunning. A complex piece, in an unusual time signature, their rendering of it lasted over 12 minutes. It was the last tune recorded and was done in one straight "take." No

*false starts or second thoughts! Right now, I can't think of
a better example of the results that can flow from the
presence of profound rapport. Nor is it easy to think of a
project that could have gone so disastrously wrong in the
absence of such rapport.*

The foregoing chapters in this book have discussed how
to set about devising and delivering therapeutic metaphors. This one will discuss what not to do.

Metaphor can be very powerful. It can also fall flat.
Although it may not matter that the intended message was
not actually received, the telling of stories that are boring
or are regarded by clients as irrelevant, may do damage to
the therapeutic relationship. As long as the story, anecdote, or task interests the client and strengthens engage-
ment, it is at least of some value. The most important thing
is not to "lose" the client.

SOME COMMON PITFALLS

The following are some pitfalls to avoid:

1. Attempting to use metaphorical methods before adequate rapport exists

Proceeding when there is insufficient rapport may be
the greatest single cause of failure, not only when metaphor is the therapeutic device being used, but also when
any other indirect or strategic methods are attempted. (It is
also a major cause of failure in such other human endeavors as selling and teaching.) Although I have pointed out
the importance of rapport in earlier sections of this book,
I make no apology for bringing it up again here. When
rapport is really well developed, you need have no fear
that your metaphor will be consciously rejected, or even
questioned, however strange your choosing to tell a story
at the particular juncture might seem to those who are not
in rapport with you.

Remember the blind obedience, referred to in Chapter 6, that the followers of Jim Jones in Guyana and David Koresh at Waco, Texas, displayed. The rapport that Jones had with his followers was strong enough that several hundred willingly drank cyanide when he told them to. A happier example of rapport, leading to positive results, is the anecdote at the beginning of this chapter. Jazz is an improvised music, though it usually starts with a framework upon which the musicians improvise. Rapport between the musicians is generally a *sine qua non* of a good performance. The history of jazz music is rich with examples of bands that fell apart, and performances in which the potential of the musicians was not fully realized, apparently because rapport between the members was lacking.

In our clinical work, we must pay as much attention to the establishment and maintaining of rapport as those in any other field of human activity involving relationships between people need to do.

2. Offering a major metaphorical intervention before a proper assessment has been completed

We have seen that a careful assessment is necessary before a therapy plan is instituted. This should include a carefully taken history. The value of knowing your client well cannot be overemphasized. This may sound like stating the obvious, but the therapist struck by a great idea for a metaphor—or other therapeutic maneuver—may be tempted to go ahead and use this before acquiring an adequate understanding of the client's condition. You would not expect a surgeon to proceed with an operation without first reviewing the patient's past medical history and carrying out a careful assessment of the patient's current condition. To do so would be regarded as bad practice. Similar considerations apply to psychotherapy. The need for a proper assessment is related also to the matters discussed in the next section.

3. Choosing a story or activity to which your client has unpleasant, fear-filled, or otherwise negative associations

We need to know our clients well before devising specific therapeutic strategies. For similar reasons, physicians and pharmacists, before prescribing or dispensing drugs, usually ask their patients if they suffer from any allergies or have had any adverse reactions to drugs in the past.

Many of our clients have had bad reactions—not to drugs (though they may have had these too) but to particular situations or activities. For example, a person who has had an experience of nearly drowning while at the seaside, or one who has lost a close relative or friend through drowning in the sea, might well react adversely to a story set in a seaside location. Yet many people have happy associations with the seaside. So we need to know just whom we are dealing with before we devise our story or anecdote.

Again, if an objective of a metaphor is to mobilize emotional resources, using a metaphor that brings to mind an event or experience in which the subject's emotional resources proved insufficient may not be helpful. It might even have a detrimental effect, as a result of its association with failure on a previous occasion. (This does not mean that metaphor cannot be used to deal with the emotional aftermath of such events, but that is a different matter.)

4. Overlooking the importance of some aspect of the real-life situation to which you intend to apply the metaphor

This is really just another way of saying that a proper assessment is necessary before you devise and offer your "therapeutic" metaphor; without it, your metaphor may prove not to be therapeutic. It is advisable to list, at least in your mind if not on paper, all the key elements of the clinical situation in which you plan to offer your story, task, or other metaphorical vehicle. Then check through to make sure that all are covered.

5. Allowing insufficient time for delivery of the metaphor

Not allowing enough time for delivery of a metaphor can predispose to failure. I like to be generous in the time I allow myself, so that I can tell my story, or describe the task or ritual in a leisurely way with no feeling of the need to hurry. This may seem to be at odds with the desirability, mentioned in the previous chapter, of leaving major meta-phorical inputs until near the end of the session. There certainly are advantages to leaving only a limited amount of time between the end of the story (or whatever the metaphorical medium is) and the end of the session.

One way of avoiding the pressure that can come from knowing that another client is waiting to see you, if you take longer than you expected, is to see those to whom you plan to offer a major metaphor at the end of your working day. I find that this open-ended situation gives me the flexibility I value.

6. Starting before clear therapeutic goals have been agreed upon with your client(s)

The importance of establishing clear goals, agreed upon with your clients, has been pointed out in previous chap-ters. While there is no reason why therapists should not use anecdotes and brief stories with metaphorical mean-ings at any point, when major metaphors designed to produce change or reframe situations in significant, planned ways are developed, this should only be done in the context of agreed objectives.

7. Failing to choose the right metaphors and overlooking the metaphors clients are offering

It is important to note the metaphors used by your clients. Do they process information using primarily the visual, auditory, or kinesthetic sensory channels? Are they concerned with rural or urban scenarios? When your clients are children, what do they like to play with? The girl who likes to play with dolls, as most do, may be most open to stories or play featuring dolls. The boy whose principal interest proves to be in sports in which teams vie for supremacy may find metaphors about championship play-offs or games in which players adopted particular roles especially meaningful.

I have found that many aggressive boys are fascinated by video games in which conflicts are enacted. These, and also some T.V. or newspaper cartoons, may be used as metaphors for the battles they are having with their parents or siblings or others in their lives.

THE IMPORTANCE OF OBSERVING
FEEDBACK

The effective therapist is always keenly observing the feedback—especially the nonverbal feedback—being offered by his or her clients. Is your client attending to what you are saying or doing, rather than looking around the room or glancing at the clock on the wall? Does the subject matter you are talking about seem to interest the client? Does your client understand what you are saying? We therapists tend to have high levels of education and it is easy to "talk over the heads" of clients who have a less advanced level of learning. This applies with special force to children.

Clinicians who are still learning about how to work with children can easily misjudge the level at which they need to pitch the stories or anecdotes they tell their child clients. It is a good idea to ask children for feedback if you are in any doubt about whether they are "with" you. It is quite in order to ask, "Do you know what a desert island is?" if you are talking about a desert island. There are some words that seem quite simple—"strict" is one—that many children do not understand. So keep a wary eye open for signs that your child clients (and your grown up ones, too) are looking puzzled or just blank. When that happens, it is well to check out with them whether they are understanding you. Doing so, in a respectful manner, often helps solidify rapport.

Further information about interview techniques for use with children may be found in *Clinical Interviews with Children and Adolescents* (Barker, 1990).

RECTIFYING MISTAKES

It is inevitable that you will, from time to time, make what turns out to have been an unfortunate choice of metaphor, anecdote, or task. I remember once, in the course of a hypnotherapy session, telling a patient a story that involved mention of a dungeon. Often clients will come out of trance when something that has negative connotations is mentioned. On this occasion, though, my patient did not do so. Her ideomotor responses suggested to me that something important was happening. On reorientation, she said that the experience had been "horrible" because she had long had a fear of dungeons, stemming from experiences of being confined by an abusive father when she was a child. This problem could probably have been avoided if I had taken a more comprehensive history, but I had missed this particular point.

This patient was quite reluctant to engage in further hypnotherapy and it was not until several sessions later that she was willing to resume this. In the meantime, I first apologized to her for what was indubitably my mistake, and then went on to explore in detail what were the experiences that I should avoid in future sessions. Interestingly, when she did resume hypnotherapy, we were, with the patient's permission, able to explore and deal with her fear of confinement.

SUMMARY

Pitfalls to be avoided in using metaphors include starting before sufficient rapport exists; failing to make a proper preliminary assessment of the case; choosing a scenario with which your client has unpleasant associations; allowing insufficient time; starting before goals have been agreed upon; and choosing an unsuitable metaphorical medium.

Observing the feedback—especially nonverbal—that clients offer is important; overlooking this can lead to therapeutic failure. When mistakes are made or metaphors that prove to be unsuitable are offered, the situation is likely to get worse if active steps to rectify the mistake(s) are not promptly taken.

10

ETHICAL CONSIDERATIONS

THE DIFFICULTY OF DOING THINGS RIGHT
FOR EVERYONE

In the heat of the day, a father went through the dusty streets of Keshan with his son and a donkey. The father sat on the donkey, and the boy led it. "The poor kid," said a passerby. "His short little legs try to keep up with the donkey. How can that man sit there so lazily on the donkey when he sees that the boy is running himself ragged?" The father took this comment to heart, climbed down from the donkey at the next corner, and let the boy climb up.

But it wasn't long before another passerby raised his voice and said, "What a disgrace! The little brat sits up there like a sultan, while his poor old father runs along-side." This remark hurt the boy very much, and he asked his father to sit behind him on the donkey.

"Have you ever seen anything like that," griped a veiled woman. "Such cruelty to animals. The donkey's back is sagging, and that good-for-nothing and his son lounge around as if it were a divan—the poor creature!"

The targets of this criticism looked at each other and, without saying a word, climbed down from the donkey. But they had barely gone a few steps when a stranger poked fun at them by saying, "Thank heavens I'm not that stupid. Why do you two walk your donkey when he doesn't do you any good, when he doesn't even carry one of you?"

The father shoved a handful of straw into the donkey's mouth and laid his hand on his son's shoulder. "Regardless of what we do," he said, "there's someone who disagrees with it. I think we have to know for ourselves what we think is right."

This story, from *Oriental Stories as Tools in Psychotherapy* (Peseschkian, 1986), is not intended to make any kind of definitive statement about ethical issues in the use of therapeutic metaphors, though it does make the valid point that there is more than one way of looking at just about anything. This applies to ethical issues, the rights and wrongs of which are not always clear.

I have two reasons for quoting the above tale. The first is that I like it and have found it useful, usually modified in some way, in various clinical situations. So I needed to find an excuse to reproduce it in this book. But secondly, the story makes two worthwhile and important points. One, of course, is that there is more than one way of looking at things—at anything. The other is that it is hard to live one's life depending on the opinions of others about what one should do. This is something that many people, especially those who harbor feelings of insecurity and low self-worth, tend to do.

THE ETHICS OF STRATEGIC THERAPY

It is generally agreed that everything we do in the course of our clinical work must be done, and should only be done, with the informed consent of our respective clients. But what does this mean when applied to strategic methods of therapy? Must we explain our planned strategies before we start? And if we did, would they work? Probably most of them would not.

The ethical question might be seen as that of deciding whether "the end justifies the means" in clinical situations such as those with which psychotherapists deal. This question may be asked of any strategic, or indirect intervention. The use of metaphors is but one class of such interventions, and it is by no means the most "indirect." The strategic intervention that might be considered the most questionable is the use of paradoxical injunctions. If they are ethical—used properly in appropriate clinical situations, of course—then surely the use of metaphors should present no problem! While it is not an example of the use of metaphor, but rather of an even more "strategic" device, let us consider the following case:

> The parents of a 15-year-old girl sought help because they could not get her to go to school. She had become pregnant and had had an abortion three months previously. This occurred during the summer school holiday period. When the time came for her to return to school in the fall, she said she did not yet feel quite ready to resume her studies. It was therefore decided that she could have a further one month to "convalesce." But at the end of this time she was still reluctant to return. She did attend school intermittently for a few weeks, but attendance then tailed off until she was not going at all.
>
> When I met the family I discovered that Gillian was spending most of her time at home with her mother, while the father, a financially successful businessman, was working long hours, and was often away from home for several days at a time. I also discovered that an older sister had become pregnant at age 16 and had had an abortion about two years previously. This had upset the mother more than enough, but having a second daughter who got into the same situation seemed to have devastated her. It had left her quite depressed. Moreover she had apparently had little support from her husband, who generally left the care of the children and the home to his wife.

The intervention I offered the family was as follows:

"Mrs. F, you have been through a very harrowing time. Both your daughters have become pregnant as teenagers and have had abortions. You have stood loyally by them and this has been, and continues to be, a great strain on you.

"Mr. F, I admire the tireless way you work to ensure a good life for your family. You are an outstanding businessman with many responsibilities. With such a heavy burden of work it is just not possible for you to spend as much time at home supporting your family as I am sure you would wish to do.

"Gillian, you have been sensitive to your mother's distress and feelings of depression and have felt her need for your support and companionship while your father is away so much.

[*To the parents*] "Important as school undoubtedly is, I think it is too early for Gillian to return to school. While her mother remains as upset as she clearly is, and since you cannot be with her, Mr. F, I think it is better if Gillian stays at home for a while."

Mr. F was not impressed with my suggestions. The next day, displaying unprecedented interest in his daughter's situation, he took time off from work, told Gillian to come with him to the school, marched her into the principal's office, and demanded her reinstatement. (She had been "suspended" for non-attendance). The principal agreed that Gillian could return if she undertook to attend regularly. Mr. F said he would see that she did.

Starting the following day, Gillian attended school regularly and Mr. F was reported to be spending more time at home and was seen as being more of a support to his wife. The only "problem" was that he thought, from the moment I offered it, that my advice was both stupid and ridiculous. His opinion of psychiatrists, which had never been high, had sunk even lower!

In the above case, an intervention was offered that ostensibly "told" the clients to do the opposite of what they seemed to need to do to resolve their problem. If it was ethical, then surely metaphor, which usually offers suggestions, ideas, interpretations or reframings that might be offered—and, indeed, may already have been unsuccessfully offered—in direct ways, presents no real ethical problem.

Was my intervention ethical? It seemingly was not done with the informed consent generally considered something ethical practitioners should obtain. In a sense, the family, especially the father, was "tricked" into getting the girl back into school. Nevertheless, this single session, done as a consultation to another therapist, yielded results that were exactly those the parents had been requesting. The daughter returned to school, as they wanted her to do.

I can tell you that on this subject my conscience feels clear. In my opinion, my intervention was entirely ethical. By using what some might call a manipulative device, I enabled the family to take the steps necessary to solve their problem. And not only did the daughter return to school, but in addition the father began to give more support to his wife.

I believe that the use of strategic devices is ethically entirely acceptable if it is done with the aim of the meeting the goals previously agreed between therapist and client(s). I do not think that our clients need to understand, or even be told, of the technicalities of the therapeutic process, just as a man having his gallbladder removed does not have to know the technical details of a cholecystectomy. What he does need is, first, full confidence in the surgeon; and secondly a general understanding of what is to be done— removal of an infected gallbladder full of gallstones, perhaps. The risks of the operation and the possible adverse results need to be explained also, and there should be a full discussion of the balance of risks and benefits associated with the procedure.

A similar clarification of objectives and any possible drawbacks to the treatment is necessary when psychotherapy is the treatment to be used, as we have seen in Chapter 6. In the case of Gillian and her parents, all these requirements had received attention and were, I believe, met. One might go even further and argue that it would be unethical to fail to use a strategic approach in a case such as this. A lot of work with the family had been done by another therapist who had used more direct methods. These had not yielded the desired results, so would it be good practice to try more of the same? And if it is not good practice, can it be ethical?

We might also raise the question of whether it is our conscious or our unconscious minds that must give informed consent. Metaphors speak to the unconscious. Is it ethical to inform the conscious mind, when it is the unconscious mind that really needs the information, the ideas, the alternative ways of looking at the situation, the possible solutions, that the metaphor is designed to convey?

It is difficult to know just what the unconscious mind is experiencing and doing when we offer metaphors or other material. My own experience, though, is that therapeutic suggestions that are unacceptable are either ignored—the most common response—or overtly rejected.

The reported work of Milton Erickson is replete with unconventional interventions. Nowadays, many of these might be regarded as of questionable ethical propriety. Erickson would stage a meal in a restaurant and rehearse the waiter ahead of time on what to do and say; he had people climbing Squaw Peak, a mountain in Phoenix; and he even told a man to drive as far as he could on a road out of the city and then get out and lie in the ditch when he felt faint—as he was prone to feel when driving beyond the city limits.

Many of these tasks seem to have had a metaphorical meaning, though they also had other properties. Were they ethical? It does not seem that Erickson's ethics were ever questioned, perhaps because he so obviously had his patients' best interests at heart. And that, surely, is the essence of this question. Is what you do planned with your clients' best interests as the prime consideration? As long as it is, and you can demonstrate this, I believe you have nothing to fear. This is especially so if you take proper care to establish and maintain a deep degree of rapport.

SUMMARY

The ethical issues involved in the use of therapeutic metaphors are not essentially different from those arising in the course of other forms of practice. In using metaphor, they may even be fewer than those that arise in other forms of strategic therapy.

Necessary safeguards include the establishment of clear, agreed on goals before treatment starts; the existence of a clearly understood—though not necessarily written—contract to the effect that all the efforts of the therapist will be directed towards achieving the agreed goals; and the absolute imperative that the therapist at all times consider the best interests of the clients as his or her primary concern.

Clients are unlikely to question your ethics if the above criteria are met and, in addition, good rapport with them is maintained at all times.

RECOMMENDED READING*

BOOKS DEALING SPECIFICALLY WITH THERAPEUTIC METAPHORS

Barker, P. (1985). *Using Metaphors in Psychotherapy.* Provides a systematic account of the theory and practice of using therapeutic metaphors and offers examples for use in a variety of clinical situations.

Gordon, D. (1978). *Therapeutic Metaphors.* Strongly influenced by neuro-linguistic programming; offers an in-depth account of how to construct a major metaphorical story for a specific clinical problem.

Kopp, R. R. (1995). *Metaphor Therapy: Using Client-Generated Metaphors in Psychotherapy.* Discusses how therapists may use their clients' own metaphors in a variety of types of therapy. Contains much practical advice.

Kopp, S. (1971). *Guru: Metaphors from a Psychotherapist.* A thought-provoking book which discusses, with

*Full bibliographic details can be found in the references.

147

many examples, how material from a wide variety of cultures may be used in the creation of metaphors for clinical problems,

Lankton, S., & Lankton, C. (1983). *The Answer Within: A Clinical Framework of Ericksonian Hypnotherapy.* Heavily influenced by the work of Milton Erickson; includes an extensive account, with case examples of how to use multiple embedded metaphors.

Mills, J., & Crowley, R. (1986). *Therapeutic Metaphors for Children and the Child Within.* Influenced strongly by the work of Milton Erickson and by neuro-linguistic programming; offers many creative ways of using metaphors. Valuable sections on artistic metaphors and cartoon therapy, with illustrations.

Peseschkian, N. (1986). *Oriental Stories as Tools in Psychotherapy.* Discusses the use of stories in psychotherapy, using tales from the Orient as examples.

Rosenblatt, P. C. (1994). *Metaphors of Family Systems Theory: Toward New Constructions.* Family therapists will find this book of interest as it discusses the role of metaphors for family systems and various aspects of their functioning.

SOURCES OF METAPHORICAL MATERIAL

Brett, D. (1988). *Annie Stories: A Special Kind of Storytelling.*

Brett, D. (1992). *More Annie Stories: Therapeutic Storytelling Techniques.*

Hague, M. (Ed.). (1993). *The Rainbow Fairy Book* (A collection of some of the best of Lang's fairy tales).

Hammond, C. D. (Ed.). (1990). *Handbook of Hypnotic Suggestions and Metaphors.*

Imber-Black, E., Roberts, J., & Whiting, R. (Eds.). (1988). *Rituals in Families and Family Therapy.*

Lakoff, G., & Johnson, M. (1980). *Metaphors We Live By.*

Lang, A. *Blue Fairy Book* (1889/1965); *Red Fairy Book*

(1890/1978); *Green Fairy Book* (1892/1978); *Crimson Fairy Book* (1903/1951); *Brown Fairy Book* (1904/1966); *Lilac Fairy Book* (1910/1968).

Lankton, C., & Lankton, S. (1989). *Tales of Enchantment: Goal-Oriented Metaphors for Adults and Children in Therapy.*

Ritterman, M. (1983). *Using Hypnosis in Family Therapy.*

Sideman, B. B. (Ed.). (1967). *The World's Best Fairy Tales* (Volumes 1 and 2).

Wallas, L. (1985). *Stories for the Third Ear: Using Hypnotic Fables in Psychology.*

White, M., & Epston, D. (1990). *Narrative Means to Therapeutic Ends.*

Zeig, J., & Gilligan, S. (Eds.). (1990). *Brief Therapy: Myths, Methods and Metaphors.* (Especially Chapter 19, by Kay F. Thompson.)

OTHER ERICKSONIAN RESOURCES

Milton Erickson's work contains much that is relevent to the use of therapeutic metaphors. The following are among the books available:

Haley, J. (1973). *Uncommon Therapy: The Psychiatric Techniques of Milton H. Erickson, M.D.*

O'Hanlon, W. H., & Hexum, A. L. (1990). *An Uncommon Casebook: The Complete Clinical Work of Milton H. Erickson, M.D.*

Rosen, S. (Ed.). (1982). *My Voice Will Go With You: The Teaching Tales of Milton H. Erickson, M.D.*

Rossi, E. L. (Ed.). (1980). *The Collected Papers of Milton H. Erickson* (Volumes 1 to 4).

Rossi, E. L., Ryan, M. O., & Sharp, F. A. (Eds.) (1983). *Healing in Hypnosis* (Volume 1 of the Seminars, Workshops and Lectures of Milton H. Erickson).

Rossi, E. L., & Ryan, M. O. (Eds.) (1985). *Life Reframing in Hypnosis.* (Volume 2 of the Seminars, Workshops and Lectures of Milton H. Erickson).

SOME PAPERS OF INTEREST

Atwood, J. D., & Levine, L. B. (1991). Ax murderers, dragons, spiders and webs: Therapeutic metaphors in couples therapy. *Contemporary Family Therapy, 13,* 201–217.

Briggs, J. R. (1992). Traveling indirect routes to enjoy the scenery: Employing the metaphor in family therapy. *Journal of Family Psychotherapy, 3,* 39–52.

Dolan, Y. M. (1985). Metaphor for motivation and intervention. *Family Therapy Collections, 19,* 1–10.

Groth-Marnat, G. (1992). Past traditions of therapeutic metaphor. *Psychology, 29,* 40–47.

Lenrow, P. (1966). Use of metaphor in facilitating constructive behavior change. *Psychotherapy: Theory, Reserarch and Practice, 3,* 145–148.

Muran, J. C., & Di Giuseppe, R. A. (1990). Towards a cognitive formulation of metaphor use in psychotherapy. *Clinical Psychology Review, 10,* 69–85.

Reider, N. (1972). Metaphors as interpretation. *International Journal of Psycho-Analysis, 53,* 463–469.

Santostefano, S. (1985). Metaphor: Integrating action, fantasy and language in development. *Imagination, Cognition and Personality, 4,* 127–146.

REFERENCES

Atwood, J. D., & Levine, L. B. (1991). Ax murderers, dragons, spiders and webs: Therapeutic metaphors in couples therapy. *Contemporary Family Therapy, 13*, 201–217.

Bandler, R. (1984). *Magic in action.* Cupertino, CA: Meta Publications.

Bandler, R., & Grinder, J. (1975a). *Patterns of the hypnotic techniques of Milton H. Erickson, Volume 1.* Cupertino, CA: Meta Publications.

Bandler, R., & Grinder, J. (1975b). *The structure of magic, Volume 1.* Palo Alto, CA: Science and Behavior Books.

Bandler, R., & Grinder, J. (1979). *Frogs into princes.* Moab, UT: Real People Press.

Bandler, R., & Grinder, J. (1982). *Reframing: Neuro-linguistic programming and the transformation of meaning.* Moab, UT: Real People Press.

Barker, P. (1985). *Using metaphors in psychotherapy.* New York: Brunner/Mazel.

Barker, P. (1990). *Clinical interviews with children and adolescents.* New York: Norton.

Barker, P. (1992). *Basic family therapy* (3rd. ed.). Oxford, England: Blackwell; New York: Oxford.

Barker, P. (1994). Reframing: The essence of psychotherapy? In J. K. Zeig (Ed.), *Ericksonian methods: The essence of the story* (pp. 211–223). New York: Brunner/Mazel.

Bethel, T. (1977). *George Lewis: A jazzman from New Orleans*. Berkeley, CA: University of California Press.

Brett, D. (1988). *Annie stories: A special kind of storytelling.* New York: Workman.

Brett, D. (1992). *More Annie stories: Therapeutic storytelling techniques*. New York: Magination Press.

Briggs, J. R. (1992). Traveling indirect routes to enjoy the scenery: Employing the metaphor in family therapy. *Journal of Family Psychotherapy, 3,* 39–52.

Coppersmith, E. I. (1981). Developmental reframing. *Journal of Strategic and Systemic Therapies, 1,* 1–8.

DiLeo, J. H. (1983). *Interpreting children's drawings*. New York: Brunner/Mazel.

Dilts, R., Grinder, J., Bandler, R., Bandler, L. C., & DeLozier, J. (1980). *Neuro-linguistic programming: The study of the structure of subjective experience, Volume 1*. Cupertino, CA: Meta Publications.

Dolan, Y. M. (1985). Metaphor for motivation and intervention. *Family Therapy Collections, 19,* 1–10.

Erickson, M. H., Hershman, S., & Secter, I. I. (1961). *The practical application of medical and dental hypnosis*. Chicago: Seminars on Hypnosis.

Frankl, V. (1960). Paradoxical intention: A logotherapeutic technique. *American Journal of Psychotherapy, 40,* 520–535.

Good news bible. (1976). Toronto: Canadian Bible Society.

Gordon, D. (1978). *Therapeutic metaphors*. Cupertino, CA: Meta Publications.

Grinder, J., & Bandler, R. (1976). *The structure of magic, Volume 2*. Palo Alto, CA: Science and Behavior Books.

Grinder, J., & Bandler, R. (1981). *Trance-formations: Neuro-linguistic programming and the structure of hypnosis*. Moab, UT: Real People Press.

Grinder, J., DeLozier, J., & Bandler, R. (1977). *Patterns of the hypnotic techniques of Milton H. Erickson, Volume 2*. Cupertino, CA: Meta Publications.

Groth-Marnat, G. (1992). Past traditions of therapeutic metaphor. *Psychology, 29,* 40–47.

Guillory, I. (1988). Quotation from the insert of *Queen Ida: Caught in the act*. [CD]. Hollywood, CA: GNP Crescendo Records.

Hague, M. (Ed.). (1993). *The rainbow fairy book*. New York: Morrow.

Haley, J. (1973). *Uncommon therapy: The psychiatric techniques of Milton H. Erickson, M.D.* New York: Norton.

Hammond, C. D. (Ed.). (1990). *Handbook of hypnotic suggestions and metaphors.* New York: Norton.

Hammond, C. D. (Ed.). (1992). *Hypnotic induction and suggestion: An introductory manual.* Des Plaines, IL: American Society of Clinical Hypnosis.

Imber-Black, E., Roberts, J., & Whiting, R. (Eds.). (1988). *Rituals in families and family therapy.* New York: Norton.

Jones, M., & Chilton, J. (1971). *Louis.* London: Studio Vista.

Karpel, M. A., & Strauss, E. S. (1983). *Family evaluation.* New York: Gardner Press.

Kopp, R. R. (1995). *Metaphor therapy: Using client-generated metaphors in psychotherapy.* New York: Brunner/Mazel.

Kopp, S. (1971). *Guru: Metaphors from a psychotherapist.* Palo Alto, CA: Science and Behavior Books.

Kopp, S. B. (1972). *If you meet the Buddha on the road, kill him!: The pilgrimage of psychotherapy patients.* Palo Alto, CA: Science and Behavior Books.

Lakoff, G., & Johnson, M. (1980). *Metaphors we live by.* Chicago: University of Chicago Press.

Lang, A. (1951). *Crimson fairy book.* London: Longman Group. (Original work published by Longman Green, London, 1903, subsequent printings as a Kestral Book).

Lang, A. (1965). *Blue fairy book.* New York: Dover. (Original work published by Longman Green, London, 1889).

Lang, A. (1966). *Brown fairy book.* New York: McGraw-Hill. (Original work published by Longman Green, London, 1904; also republished by Dover, New York, 1965).

Lang, A. (1968). *Lilac fairy book.* New York: Dover. (Original work published by Longman Green, London, 1910).

Lang, A. (1978a). *Green fairy book.* New York: Viking Press. (Original work published by Longman Green, London, 1892).

Lang, A. (1978b). *Red fairy book.* New York: Viking Press. (Original work published by Longman Green, London, 1890).

Lankton, C., & Lankton, S. (1989). *Tales of enchantment: Goal-oriented metaphors for adults and children in therapy.* New York: Brunner/Mazel.

Lankton, S. (1980). *Practical magic: A translation of basic neuro-linguistic programming into clinical psychotherapy.* Cupertino, CA: Meta Publications.

Lankton, S., & Lankton, C. (1983). *The answer within: A clinical framework of Ericksonian hypnotherapy.* New York: Brunner/Mazel.

Lenrow, P. (1966). Use of metaphor in facilitating constructive behavior change. *Psychotherapy: Theory, Research and Practice, 3,* 145–148.

Madanes, C. (1981). *Strategic family therapy.* San Francisco: Jossey-Bass.

Mills, J. C., & Crowley, R. J. (1986). *Therapeutic metaphors for children and the child within.* New York: Brunner/Mazel.

Minuchin, S. (1974). *Families and family therapy.* Cambridge, MA: Harvard University Press.

Monroe, B. (1994, April 26). Interview. *Calgary Herald.*

Muran, J. C., & DiGiuseppe, R. A. (1990). Towards a cognitive formulation of metaphor use in psychotherapy. *Clinical Psychology Review, 10,* 69–85.

O'Hanlon, W. H., & Hexum, A. L. (1990). *An uncommon casebook: The complete clinical work of Milton H. Erickson, M.D.* New York: Norton.

Orwell, G. (1945). *Animal farm: A fairy story.* London: Secker and Warburg.

Palazzoli, M. S., Boscolo, L., Cecchin, G., & Prata, G. (1978). *Paradox and counterparadox.* New York: Jason Aronson.

Papp, P. (1980). The Greek chorus and other techniques of paradoxical therapy. *Family Process, 19,* 45–57.

Papp, P. (1982). Staging reciprocal metaphors in a couples group. *Family Process, 21,* 453–467.

Peseschkian, N. (1986). *Oriental stories as tools in psychotherapy.* Berlin: Springer-Verlag. (Originally published in German as *Der Kaufman und der Papagei* by Fischer Taschenbuch, Frankfurt am Main, 1979; and in English as *The Merchant and the Parrot* by Vantage Press, New York, 1982.)

Ritterman, M. (1983). *Using hypnosis in family therapy.* San Francisco: Jossey-Bass.

Rosen, S. (Ed.). (1982). *My voice will go with you: The teaching tales of Milton H. Erickson, M.D.* New York: Norton.

Rosenberg, D. (1986). *World mythology: An anthology of the great myths and epics.* Lincolnwood, IL: National Textbook.

Rosenblatt, P. C. (1994). *Metaphors of family systems theory: Toward new constructions.* New York: Guilford.

Rossi, E. L. (Ed.). (1980). *The collected papers of Milton H. Erickson* (Vols. 1–4). New York: Irvington.

Rossi, E. L. (1985). *Dreams and the growth of personality: Expanding awareness in psychotherapy* (2nd. ed). New York: Brunner/Mazel.

Rossi, E. L., Ryan, M. O., & Sharp, F. A. (Eds.). (1983). *Healing in hypnosis.* (Volume 1 of the Seminars, Workshops and Lectures of Milton H. Erickson.) New York: Irvington.

Rossi, E. L., & Ryan, M. O. (Eds.). (1985). *Life reframing in hypnosis.* (Volume 2 of the Seminars, Workshops and Lectures of Milton H. Erickson.) New York: Irvington.

Sideman, B. B. (Ed.). (1967). *The world's best fairy tales* (Vols. 1–2). Pleasantville, NY: Reader's Digest Association.

Sperry, R. (1968). Hemispheric disconnection and unity of conscious awareness. *American Psychologist, 23,* 723–733.

Turbayne, C. M. (1970). *The myth of metaphor.* Columbia, SC: University of South Carolina Press.

Wallas, L. (1985). *Stories for the third ear: Using hypnotic fables in psychology.* New York: Norton.

Watzlawick, P. (1978). *The language of change.* New York: Brunner/Mazel.

White, M., & Epston, D. (1990). *Narrative means to therapeutic ends.* New York: Norton.

Zeig, J. K. (Ed.). (1980). *A teaching seminar with Milton H. Erickson.* New York: Brunner/Mazel.

Zeig, J. K., & Gilligan, S. G. (Eds.). (1990). *Brief therapy: Myths, methods and metaphors.* New York: Brunner/Mazel.

INDEX